HAVE YOU HEARD THE GOOD NEWS?

Have You Heard the Good News?

REFLECTIONS ON THE SUNDAY GOSPELS

Cycle A

EDWARD T. DOWLING, SJ

ALBA·HOUSE NEW·YORK

SOCIETY OF ST. PAUL, 2187 VICTORY BLVD., STATEN ISLAND, NEW YORK 10314

ST PAULS

Library of Congress Cataloging-in-Publication Data

Dowling, Edward T., S.J.
    Have you heard the good news? : reflections on the Sunday Gospels,
    cycle A / Edward T. Dowling.
        p. cm.
    ISBN 0-8189-0899-8 (alk. paper)
    1. Church year sermons. 2. Bible. N.T. Matthew—Sermons. 3. Bible. N.T.
Gospels—Sermons. 4. Catholic Church—Sermons. 5. Sermons, American—
21st century. I. Title.

BX1756.D69 H38 2001
252'.6—dc21

                                                              2001018210

Produced and designed in the United States of America by the
Fathers and Brothers of the Society of St. Paul,
2187 Victory Boulevard, Staten Island, New York 10314-6603,
as part of their communications apostolate.

ISBN: 0-8189-0899-8

Printing Information:

Current Printing - first digit   1   2   3   4   5   6   7   8   9   10

Year of Current Printing - first year shown

2001   2002   2003   2004   2005   2006   2007   2008   2009   2010

Table of Contents

Table of Contents

Preface

This collection of homilies represents the fruit of thirty years of preaching each Sunday in parishes in the Bronx, Westchester, and Long Island. People from very different social, racial, and educational backgrounds have all claimed to have enjoyed these sermons and to have profited from them. Their enthusiastic response and desire to know more about the Good News provided the motivating force behind this publication. It is my hope that these homilies will help people to understand Scripture better, appreciate it more, and read it more frequently. This book is intended for everyone who would like to be better acquainted with the Sunday readings, not merely the homilist in search of ideas for his next sermon.

I feel I should start with a disclaimer. Let me explain why. In my first twenty-nine years of preaching I never wrote out a homily. I spoke simply from notes and outlines scribbled on 3" x 5" pieces of paper. There was neither thought nor room nor perceived need for proper referencing and citations. I was speaking extemporaneously and simply trying to share with the congregation what I had learned on the topic. Over all those years whenever someone asked for a copy of a homily, I had nothing to give them for I had only jottings that were unintelligible to anyone but me. It wasn't until Advent 1998 that I first began to write out my homilies. I did so in response to lay people and nuns who said they would be helped if they had a copy of the homily to reflect on. I never thought of the possibility of publication even then until the same people urged me to try.

I am one of the least creative of God's creatures; a modest man, with much to be modest about. If I have any gift, it's as a teacher helping others to understand and come to love what I have learned and love myself. This collection of homilies owes much to many people and sources over thirty years of struggling to prepare a half-way decent homily each week. Many of the sources I regretfully cannot now adequately remember or specifically acknowledge. Let me mention, however, a few of the more unforgettable helps and influences to which I am particularly indebted.

My first inspiration came from Edward Mally, SJ, my New Testament Scripture Professor in Theology. He opened up the Sacred Text for me and taught me an approach that I have tried to emulate to this day. For the next fifteen years of preaching I muddled through pretty much on my own. Then in 1984 while helping out as a civilian chaplain to the U.S. Army in Germany, I came upon a copy of *Share the Word* whose editor at the time, Laurence F.X. Brett, was absolutely brilliant in explaining the Sunday readings, both Old and New Testaments. Each of his monthly installments helped me tremendously but I am unable now to document that help because my copies of the magazine have long since been discarded. The magazine is still a gem, however, and warrants attention.[1]

In 1995 a parish priest friend introduced me to *Homily Helps* from St. Anthony's Messenger Press.[2] They have a series of reflections for both Sundays and weekdays, each of which includes sections on scriptural exegesis as well. I find the exegetical sections for weekdays particularly helpful and informative. At about the same time another priest friend told me of Mark Link's two volumes, *Illustrated Sunday Homilies*, both of which are excellent.[3] He is a master story teller whom I have used over and over but

---

[1] *Share the Word*, Paulist National Catholic Evangelization Association, 3031 Fourth Street NE, Washington, DC 20017-1102.

[2] *Homily Helps* and *Weekday Homily Helps*, St. Anthony Messenger Press, 1615 Republic Street, Cincinnati, OH 45210.

[3] Mark Link, SJ, *Illustrated Sunday Homilies*, Tabor Publishing, 200 E. Bethany Dr., Allen, TX 75002.

whose stories I have tried to eliminate where possible from the current collection. Nevertheless, people always love a good story and I can say from experience that his stories can be used effectively as introductions, conclusions, or illustrations to many of these homilies. A treasure trove for explanations and background material on both the Old and New Testaments is William Barclay's *The Daily Study Bible Series.*[4] It is suitable for both the homilist and lay person. Though all seventeen volumes are good, the six volumes on the Gospels are perhaps the most practical.

In the past few years two Jesuit friends have also shared their homilies with me. I have enjoyed and profited from their work and would like to acknowledge and thank them both: Gus Grady, SJ, has a private publication, *Searching the Sunday Scriptures*, and Bill O'Malley, SJ, a prolific author, offers a homily each week that is aimed at college students.

---

[4] William Barclay, *The Daily Study Bible Series*, Westminster Press, 100 Witherspoon St., Louisville, KY 40202.

A Thief in the Night

Jesus gave us many beautiful images of himself: the light of the world; the bread of life; the way, the truth, and the life. In today's Gospel, however, he tells us he will come into the world like a thief in the night. What does he mean when he uses the image of a thief for himself?

Since today is the First Sunday of Advent and we begin a new liturgical year which will concentrate on the Gospel of Matthew, let us see how this image fits into Matthew's overall Gospel structure. In 12:22, Matthew tells us that Jesus cured a man who was both blind and mute physically. Unlike the scribes and Pharisees who were blind to God's presence in Jesus and obstinately refused to speak favorably of him, the crowds who witnessed the miracle were astonished at Jesus' power and immediately began to draw the right conclusions. "Can this be the Son of David?", they ask, echoing the very title Matthew gave to Jesus at the beginning of his Gospel (1:1).

The Pharisees, however, remain incurably blind, refusing to see the power of God at work in Jesus, and rather than remain silent or mute, declare that Jesus is acting with the help of Beelzebul, the prince of devils. Recall that at the time people thought that sickness and infirmity were the result of sin and that sick people were under the control of the devil. We see evidence of this primitive and cruel belief in the cure of the man born blind (Jn 9:1) when the disciples ask Jesus, "Rabbi, who sinned, this man or his parents, for him to have been born blind?" We also see a vestige of this misconception still prevalent today in the common practice of saying, "God bless you," when someone sneezes.

Jesus answers the Pharisees' absurd charge of his working for the devil with a short parable (12:29) which plays upon the word "Beelzebul." "Beelzebul" means literally "lord of the flies." It can

1

also be translated "lord of the house." The parable asks, "How can anyone enter a strong man's house and make off with his property unless he has first (overpowered and) tied him up?" In it Jesus makes use of the Pharisees' own conception of Satan in control of the sinner. They, like many pious Jews at the time, felt that human-kind had abrogated its control of the world through its collective sin and effectively handed it over to Satan. The only way the world could be saved from its evil ways and Satan's stranglehold on it broken was for God to intervene directly, to send a Messiah. In the words of the parable, "unless someone (overpower him and) tie him up."

By curing the blind man, who many believed to be in the power of Satan simply because of his physical affliction, Jesus showed himself more powerful than Satan, capable of overpower-ing his evil force and wresting people from his control. Like a thief in this sense, then, Jesus entered the world to rob the house of Sa-tan and free humankind from sin. Jesus came precisely to rob Sa-tan of his treasure, to despoil him of his ill-gotten gains.

The unusual image of a thief, which illuminates Jesus' cen-tral role in the history of salvation, is also used frequently in terms of the end of time. Jesus came to set us free from sin, to rescue us from Satan's power. To enjoy that freedom, we must be ready by the lives we lead to greet him when he comes, whenever he comes. Unfortunately, however, we frequently get tied up in the things of this world, as important as they are, like earning a decent living, providing for the children's education, balancing professional ad-vancement and familial obligations, setting aside a nest egg for retirement, that too often we have too little time left for God and end up compromising by taking on more of the world's ways and values. At the start of Advent the Church reminds us that we know not the hour or the day when the Lord will come to call us, and so we should always be ready, not in a sense of fear that God might pounce upon us when we are least prepared, but in a sense of love that always finds us doing his will to the best of our ability to show a simple return of love for love.

There's an interesting psychological test to help determine priorities. It simply involves using your imagination. Imagine you are told you only have five years to live. Sit down and make a list of what you would want to do with those five years. You can end the test there by resolving to put into practice the things you have written down. If they are the things you truly would want to do in the last years of your life, you should start doing them now because you don't know how many years you have left. But if you have the courage, you can also keep the test going to hone your list of priorities. Simply repeat the list of things you would want to do under shorter and shorter time horizons: a year, a month, a week, a day, a few minutes. As time gets shorter, the list gets shorter, revealing your true priorities. More and more things will disappear and fewer and fewer people will remain. The shorter the time, the more God and family dominate the list. And if this be true, they are the very ones we should concentrate on now. To help us prepare, the Church asks us during Advent to do something extra: go to Mass more often, be more charitable at home and work, visit the sick or the elderly, be more mindful of the poor and suffering here and abroad, deny ourselves some legitimate pleasures to make more of our resources available for those without.

The Coming of John the Baptist

The Second Sunday of Advent features the coming of John the Baptist. At the time of John the Baptist there had not been a prophet or prophetic voice in Israel for over 400 years. When John swept upon the scene, therefore, it was as if the heavens were opened and the word of God was once again being communicated. There was much excitement and anticipation because the Jewish people had long been expecting the Messiah.

The prophet Malachi (3:1) had foretold that God would send a messenger before the Messiah. Many believed that messenger would be Elijah himself who earlier had been taken up into heaven in a fiery chariot. 2 Kings 1:8 describes Elijah as wearing camel's hair and a leather belt. When John appeared, fresh from years of fasting and prayer in the desert, clothed in camel hair and a leather belt, many believed he was the promised Elijah. Matthew relates John's coming to Isaiah's earlier prophecy regarding "a herald's voice in the desert: prepare the way of the Lord, make straight his paths." In ancient times roads were frequently in terrible condition or simply non-existent. Before a king would begin an official visitation through his realm, he would send a herald ahead ordering the people to build new roads and repair old ones to facilitate the king's progress. With this image in mind, we can see that John's task as precursor or herald was to build and restore roads so that Jesus might more easily accomplish his mission when he came.

John was a fearless prophet who ultimately paid with his life for standing up for God's law. When King Herod entered into an unlawful union with his bother's wife, Herodias, John castigated him publicly even though he knew Herod could be vindictive and vengeful. When the scribes and Pharisees came to him to be baptized but without truly repenting of their sins, he likewise branded them a brood of vipers despite the fact they were the most powerful and influential religious leaders of the day. Like many other Jews, they saw no need of repentance because they thought their blood ties to Abraham would save them. From God's covenant with Abraham, they concluded that God loved Abraham so much he would not let any of his descendants be lost.

John was as humble and self-effacing as he was fearless. Though commonly regarded as a great prophet and possibly the Messiah himself, John freely confesses he is nothing compared to the one who will come after him. John admits that his baptism is only with water, indicating that it is only symbolic and not intrinsically effective. It was simply an outward manifestation of the person's inner desire to be forgiven, but it had no power of itself to forgive sin. By way of contrast, John tells us, the one to come after him would baptize with the Holy Spirit and fire, implying that this baptism will be effective, forgive sin and reunite people once again with God. All through their history the Jewish people longed for the time when the Spirit of God would come. In Ezekiel 36:27 we read, "I shall put my spirit in you, and help you keep my laws." What did the Jews mean by spirit?

The word "spirit" in Hebrew, *ruach,* means "breath" and breath is associated with life. When breath leaves the body, the person dies. So a new spirit is a new life in the Jewish understanding. The word, *ruach,* also means "wind" and wind is associated with power, driving sailing ships and turning windmills. In baptizing with the Spirit, Jesus will baptize with power, power to forgive sin and make us children of God. The Spirit of God is also associated with creation. It was the Spirit of God that calmed the chaos before creation of the world began. The Jews believed the same Spirit could overcome the disorder of sin in the human heart and turn it once again to the service and love of God. The Spirit of God also gives wisdom to the human heart and leads people to the truth. So all these beautiful and powerful images would be associated in the Jewish mind with baptism with the Spirit that John attributes to the baptism of Jesus.

Lastly, John's message for his contemporaries, as it is for us today, is to repent. Repentance involves three steps: (1) recognizing our sins and sinfulness, (2) turning away from our sins and sinfulness, and (3) turning back to God and asking his forgiveness and help. Repentance to the Jewish mind was almost a geographical concept. It meant realizing that one was on a path leading away from God, and with that knowledge deliberately turning around 180 degrees and proceeding in the exact opposite direction towards God himself.

Repentance is one of the main themes of Advent, the need to get ready to welcome Jesus into our hearts on the anniversary of his birth. The Church encourages us to true repentance involving an interior conversion or change of heart which leads to a better life.

The Blind See, the Lame Walk

Today's set of readings invites reflection on the connection and meaning of the first and third readings. The first reading comes from Isaiah. The book of the prophet Isaiah spans such a large number of years that Scripture scholars have concluded there must have been three Isaiahs. First Isaiah lived after the breakup of David's realm into two separate kingdoms. The ten northern tribes revolted against Solomon's son in Jerusalem and formed their own kingdom which they called Israel. The two remaining southern tribes, based around Jerusalem, took the name Judah. First Isaiah (1-39) was sent to warn both kingdoms to trust in God and not foreign alliances if they wished to be safe. The northern kingdom did not heed Isaiah's advice and formed an alliance with Syria against Assyria. The Assyrians quickly crushed the ten northern tribes of Israel and in 722 BC consigned them to a disastrous exile from which they never recovered or returned. History records them as the ten lost tribes of Israel. The two southern tribes of Judah, however, fearing the takeover designs of the northern kingdom more than the Assyrians, made a pact with the latter that spared them immediate annihilation. But it left them a vassal state of Assyria, paying heavy indemnities, moral and financial, until they were conquered by the Babylonians and similarly packed off into exile in 587 BC.

Second Isaiah (40-55) wrote during the Babylonian exile. He tried to keep the exiles' faith alive by assuring them they would return to Jerusalem if they put their faith in God. Cyrus the Great, founder of the Persian Empire, conquered the Babylonians some fifty years later and allowed the exiles to return home. The returnees were devastated, however, to find Jerusalem and the Temple completely destroyed. Third Isaiah's task (56-66) was to encourage them and help them rebuild. If they trusted in God, he told them,

God would help them now in reconstruction just as assuredly as he had freed them from exile.

Today's first reading is particularly beautiful and famous. In poetic fashion Isaiah describes the overwhelming joy the exiles will experience on returning home. Nature will bloom and be renewed. The joy will be so intense and liberating that, poetically speaking, the blind will be able to see again, the deaf will hear once more, and the lame will regain the strength in their legs. As important as their return to the Holy Land is, however, it pales next to God's greater gift of calling the people back to himself: enabling those blinded by sin or despair to look on him once more with hope, those deaf to his call to hear his words, the spiritually lame and infirm to walk more securely in the practice of their faith. In short, Isaiah prophesies of the people being once again reconciled to God, thus setting the world straight, allowing nature to bloom and the earth to come to life in peace and plenty, a prelude to messianic times.

In the Gospel reading we are told that John is in prison, sent there for condemning Herod for his unlawful union with his bother's wife. From all we know John expected an austere Messiah as described in Malachi 3:3 — one like a refiner's fire or fuller's lye who would purge sinners. When Jesus came preaching love and forgiveness for all, John was confused. Hence his question about whether or not Jesus is the Messiah. Jesus answers by reminding John of the other facet of messianic tradition, the one from Isaiah in the first reading. Jesus reminds John's envoys that what Isaiah foretold poetically is now being fulfilled physically in their midst. The blind see, the deaf hear, the lame walk. Through his miracles, Jesus has outstripped Isaiah's poetic expectations. But Jesus also mentions lepers cleansed and the dead raised to life, something Isaiah never dreamed of because leprosy and death were symbols of sin. Jesus thus informs John that he has far exceeded the wildest dreams of the greatest of the messianic prophets.

As a prophet himself, Jesus' words and actions always had a spiritual dimension. He cured the blind so that the onlookers could see he was no ordinary man and henceforth look at him with the eyes of faith. He cured the deaf so that people in attendance would open their ears to his message. He cured the lame so that the bystanders would follow him more closely. He cured leprosy, the worst physical disease of that time and itself a symbol of sin, to indicate he could also cure souls of sin. He raised to life the physically dead to show he could raise us spiritually to a new and everlasting life.

Jesus has ushered in the messianic age and issued an invitation to a totally different world order. If we follow him and his commandments of love of God and love for one another, we will truly have a new world order. We would see an end to war, bloodshed, and violence and the beginning of true peace with love, caring, and universal fellowship under our common Father. We would witness a complete and welcome reversal of the current world chaos. As Isaiah poetically expressed it in last week's first reading: we would see the wolf a guest of the lamb, the leopard lying down with the kid, the calf grazing with the lion. This is our prayer in Advent, that all people will accept Jesus and his way, that through a conversion of heart we will all open our lives to God and receive his Son into our hearts, homes, and homelands.

Joseph's Dream

The first reading from Isaiah (7:10-14) is confusing because it seems Isaiah is unreasonably short-tempered with Ahaz who humbly refuses to ask a sign from God. But nothing could be further from the truth. At a time when the Jewish people were divided into two kingdoms, Ahaz, who reigned over the two southern tribes of Judah from 735-715 BC, was under constant threat from Pekah, king of the ten northern tribes of Israel. Pekah wanted to annex the two southern tribes and form a single kingdom of all twelve tribes united with Syria against the Assyrians. Ahaz in turn wanted to form an alliance with Assyria to protect himself from Pekah. Isaiah warned them both against foreign alliances fearing it would destroy their independence and compromise their monotheistic belief in Yahweh. Pekah refused to heed Isaiah. Demonstrating more faith in Syria than in Yahweh, he forged an alliance with Syria. Besides insulting God, he infuriated Assyria which moved in, destroyed the kingdom of Israel, and sent the ten northern tribes into exile in 722 BC. In exile they lost both their religious faith and their national identity and simply disappeared from history. They are now known as the ten lost tribes of Israel.

Isaiah then offers Ahaz a sign of God's power to forestall a similar mistake. Ahaz refuses the sign because it is too late. Preferring subservience to Assyria to subjugation by Pekah, he had already inked a treaty with Assyria which would eventually make Judah a vassal state and force it to empty the Temple treasury and construct an Assyrian altar in the sanctuary. Isaiah is stung by Ahaz's hypocrisy and offers a sign despite his refusal to ask for one. Isaiah foretells that a virgin will conceive a son, a Messiah to save his people. He would be called Emmanuel, a name meaning "God is with us."

People are at times confused by this prophecy since Jesus was not given the name Emmanuel. The answer is that Emmanuel was intended simply as a throne name for the Messiah, much as monarchs assume throne names when they ascend the throne. Edward VIII of England, for instance, was baptized David and as a boy was known to the royal family as Bertie. But he chose the name Edward when he succeeded his father George V. When Elizabeth II became queen and was asked what name she wished to rule under, she is said to have immediately replied, "My own name, Elizabeth." On ascending the throne every monarch in England also automatically assumes a list of official throne names or titles, one of which is Defender of the Faith. Emmanuel was a similar title for Jesus.

In stark contrast to Ahaz, today's Gospel tells of Joseph, a man of faith, who trusted in God and put faith in his word. Today's passage gives us Matthew's account of the birth of Jesus. The word for "birth" in Greek is *genesis* and so we are reminded of the first book of the Bible where we read that the Spirit of God hovered over the water and creation began. Similarly, at the very beginning of Matthew's Gospel we are told that Jesus is to be conceived and born through the power of the Holy Spirit.

In ancient Jewish times engagement was a formal process lasting as long as a year in which the couple were considered to be husband and wife although they did not actually live together. To break such an engagement, divorce was necessary. Tradition tells us that when Joseph learned of Mary's pregnancy, he did not doubt her personally but felt unworthy to be part of God's plan and so decided to remove himself from the picture by divorcing her quietly. An angel of the Lord then appeared to him in a dream, a frequent means of divine communication in the Old Testament, and assured him he was very much in God's plan. A man of deep faith, he too submitted to God's wish and remained as companion and protector of Mary and foster father of the child Jesus.

In taking Mary as his wife, Joseph became the legal father of Jesus and by Jewish law Jesus would trace his lineage through Joseph, a lineage which went back to David himself. Also by Jewish law, the father bestows the name. Hence the angel gives Joseph the name for the child: Jesus, which means "Yahweh saves." Jesus came to save us from sin by assuming human form and living his life among us, to show us by word and example how we are to love God, and ultimately to lay down his life for us. The whole of the Gospel message can be summed up in this, the mystery of the Incarnation: God so loved the world that he sent his only begotten Son to save us.

As a descendant of David, Jesus will be called Son of David, another title for the Messiah who many Jews believed would be a powerful king like David who would save them from oppression and restore their liberty. They had little idea the Messiah would be God's own Son who would free us from sin and restore us to true freedom as children of God.

Today as we celebrate the fourth week of Advent and reflect on the readings, let us pray that we not build our hopes on material things like Ahaz but trust in God like Joseph and truly put ourselves at his disposal by putting his will into effect in our lives.

The Birth of Jesus

Luke's account of the birth of Jesus is particularly beautiful and the one most commonly associated with Christmas. Of all the evangelists he tried hardest to give a sense of history, time, and place. Since calendars were not commonplace at the time, he dates the birth of Jesus with cross references to famous people. He tells us that Jesus was born during the reign of Caesar Augustus, the powerful Roman emperor who was universally known since he ruled over most of the known world and presided over an enduring era of peace. With Antioch in Syria home to the second largest Christian population at the time he was writing, Luke also mentions that Quirinius was governor of Syria. The overlap of the two regimes narrows the time frame in which the birth of Jesus is situated and helps to date it more precisely.

But Luke is more interested in the sweep and meaning of history than merely dates. Notice how he uses history to convey his point and present his theology. He does this by starting at Rome, the hub of political and military power at the time and the most influential city of its day. He then moves swiftly to the Near East, the cradle of religions and mysticism. He takes us to Nazareth, a small town north of Jerusalem, and then to Bethlehem, a small town south of Jerusalem, deliberately skirting Jerusalem itself, the center of organized Jewish religion. Even Bethlehem quickly fades away. There is no room for them in the inn. Then we are brought suddenly to a manger in the middle of nowhere, far from the religious leaders in Jerusalem, farther still from the powerful in Rome. Luke thus dramatizes that when the Son of God comes, he comes not to the elite and mighty but to the humble and simple, ordinary folk like poor shepherds.

Notice the contrasts that fill the scene. The passage starts with reference to Caesar Augustus, the most powerful man in all the known world. His whim to conduct a census in order to enhance tax collections and facilitate military conscription uproots entire populations and sends them pell-mell back to their places of origin to register. Lodging is scarce, roads are poor, people forced to struggle — all so an emperor might better tax their income and compel their sons to enter military service. The passage ends, however, with the birth of Jesus who, as Son of God, is ruler over all people, not just the Roman Empire. Unlike Caesar, Jesus has come to serve and not to be served, to give and not to extort, to invite and not to force. Ironically, too, while Luke must initially date the birth of Jesus in terms of the reign of Caesar Augustus, all subsequent dating will eventually be done in relation to the birth of the Child born this day.

As attention finally settles on the little manger on the outskirts of Bethlehem, the whole scene suddenly shifts and we are presented with a panorama of heaven. The sky is filled with a host of heavenly angels praising God and promising peace on earth to all of good will. The sole witnesses are shepherds, commonly regarded as social outcasts and religious pariahs. They were social outcasts because only the poorest of the poor would follow the sheep as they roamed in the wild, far from the comforts of family and home. They were religious pariahs because the need never to leave the sheep untended forestalled their observance of the Sabbath law against servile work. Following the sheep as they grazed afar also kept them far from required Temple services and thwarted fulfillment of the Mosaic laws on ritual purification. With the shepherds the first witnesses to the newborn Child, it is clear that Jesus came not only to the poor but also to those who were publicly viewed as sinners. This doesn't exclude the rich but it shows that contrary to human ways wealth receives no priority or special attention in God's eyes.

Luke also fills the passage with many beautiful symbols that his original audience, steeped in the Old Testament, would readily pick up. Bethlehem literally means "house of bread." Bread in both the Old and New Testament is often used as a symbol for revelation or knowledge of God because the soul hungers to know about God as much as the body hungers for food. Knowledge of God is food or bread for the soul. On Christmas day Bethlehem truly lived up to its name of "house of bread," housing Jesus who is the perfect revelation of God. Bethlehem is also the city of David. Jesus is an heir to David and so an heir to his throne, as often foretold in Scripture. The Messiah will also be of the house of David, and Jesus is of the house of David. The angels tell the shepherds that they would find the Child wrapped in swaddling clothes. Swaddling clothes were usually considered baby clothes for the poor, but Wisdom (7:1) speaks of David's son, Solomon, being wrapped in swaddling clothes. With Solomon known the world over for his wisdom, this is another thinly veiled reference to Jesus being a font of revelation and an heir of David. Luke also tells us that Jesus was laid in a manger, a trough for feeding. This reminds us that Jesus will feed us with knowledge about God and God's ways through his own teaching, life, and example. We know he will also one day feed us with the true bread of life, the Eucharist, his Body and Blood. In the era when Jesus was born devout Jews were also praying fervently that the Day of the Lord would come. The angels tell the shepherds, "This day in David's city a savior has been born to you," indicating that the Day of the Lord had truly come.

As we reflect on Luke's account of the birth of Jesus, let us thank God for sending his Son to dwell among us so that he might show us by word and example how we are to respond to God's love.

Flight into Egypt

Today's Gospel is from Matthew. Matthew was Jewish and wrote primarily for a Jewish audience. He wanted to show his fellow Israelites that Jesus fulfills the Old Testament prophecies and follows very much in the tradition of Scripture's greatest figures. We see several instances of this in today's Gospel.

By all accounts Moses was the greatest teacher, leader, and law-giver of the Old Testament. He was born at a time when the Jews were enslaved in Egypt and Pharaoh had decreed all male Jewish children should be killed at birth lest they eventually grow up and challenge Egyptian rule. Moses' father is warned in a dream and Moses' mother puts her infant son in a basket and leaves him where Pharaoh's daughter will likely find him. Pharaoh's daughter finds the infant Moses, as his birth mother had hoped, and takes pity on the child. She adopts the baby, thereby preserving his life for God's future plan (Ex 2).

So, too, Matthew informs us, was Jesus' life threatened at birth by a mad ruler, Herod, who from fear Jesus would usurp his throne, ordered him killed. To ensure this, Herod also ordered all Jewish boys in Bethlehem under the age of two to be killed as well. But like Moses' father, Jesus' foster father, Joseph, is also warned in a dream of the impending danger and flees from Herod with the child and his mother to Egypt. Matthew introduces the Herod story here to show that, like Moses, Jesus too was threatened at birth and saved only by God's direct intervention.

In the Old Testament, Joseph, the youngest of Jacob's twelve sons, is sold into slavery in Egypt by his brothers where he rises to the position of head adviser to the Pharaoh. In that position he is later able to save his brothers and the Jewish people from starvation by providing food for them in time of famine. Matthew here implies that, like the great patriarch Joseph, Jesus too was sent into

Egypt by God's plan and that, like Joseph, Jesus too will one day feed his people at the multiplication of the loaves and fish and more importantly at the Last Supper when he will give them the life-giving bread of the Eucharist.

When the Jewish people were in slavery in Egypt, they prayed to God for deliverance. God heard their prayer and summoned Moses. God told Moses to go to the Pharaoh in his name with the message, "Let my son, Israel, go." It is the first time that the Jewish people are called Israel and God shows his special relationship to them by identifying them collectively as his son. Later Hosea will summarize the Exodus event using God's own words, "Out of Egypt I have called my son" (11:1). In today's Gospel, after the death of Herod the Great, an angel of the Lord, a surrogate for God himself, tells Joseph in a dream to take the child back to Israel. Matthew cites this as a fulfillment of Hosea's prophecy, "Out of Egypt I have called my son." But now the prophecy is fulfilled not figuratively as with the people of Israel but literally in the person of Jesus, God's only begotten Son. Matthew in effect informs us that Jesus is the new Israel, God's true Son.

Archelaus, the cruelest of Herod's sons, inherited Judea and Samaria, the two southernmost of the three provinces of the Holy Land, as well as Idumea. To steer clear of him, Joseph decides to go to Galilee, the northernmost province, and settles there in the town of Nazareth. Matthew then gives an obscure citation regarding Jesus that is hard to pinpoint: "He shall be called a Nazorean." Some say it refers to a Nazirite, a man or woman consecrated as sacred to God in a commitment that could be perpetual or temporary. Samuel (1 S 1) and Samson (Jg 13) were perpetual Nazirites. The Bible tells us they took no strong drink, ate nothing unclean, and no razor ever touched their head. St. Paul, on the other hand, is thought to have taken a temporary Nazirite vow when he had his head shaved at Cenchreae (Ac 18:18). Other commentators, however, point to a second meaning of *nazir*, which is "a bud," and see it as the fulfillment of Isaiah 11:1, "a shoot shall sprout from the stump of Jesse, and from his roots a bud shall blossom." As the adopted son of Joseph, Jesus was a descendant of Jesse, father of King David. In either instance, Jesus fulfills the prophecy perfectly.

Today is the Feast of the Holy Family. Father Theodore Hesburgh, former president of Notre Dame and one of the most influential educators of his day, once said, "The most important thing a father can do for his children is to love their mother." The same thing can be said for mothers. "The most important thing a mother can do for her children is to love their father." Similarly, "the most important thing children can do for their parents is to love their brothers and sisters." There are few things more important than family unity and all family members suffer when it is missing at any level. That's one reason why today's feast is so important. Bob Hope once quipped, "There's nothing I wouldn't do for Bing Crosby and there's nothing Bing Crosby wouldn't do for me. But that's the trouble. We don't do anything for each other." The same is too often true in family life. We frequently take those we love the most for granted and don't do nearly enough to make our love manifest. Love is proved in action, by what we say and do, by how we treat those we claim to love. So as we celebrate the Feast of the Holy Family, let us pray that all of us who have been born into a family at birth will show the respect and love for each of our family members that Jesus, Mary, and Joseph had for one another. Let us also remember that our first vocation in life is as a family member, and God will judge us one day, first and foremost, on how well we treated those whom he entrusted to us in our immediate family.

She Treasured All These Things in Her Heart

On this feast of Mary, the Mother of God, it is good to recall how devotion to Mary arose in the Church. Some Protestants and critics of the Church claim that Catholics give too much attention to Mary, practically deifying her and making her the equal of her Son, the equal of God. The first thing we must clarify, then, is the title itself. In declaring Mary to be the Mother of God, the Church states that Mary is the mother of Jesus Christ who, as the eternal Word, was God from the first moment of his conception. Mary gave Jesus human form, not his divine nature, and so Mary still remains a creature of God and is in no way the equal of God or her Son. She is, however, by her divinely-appointed role as Mother of Jesus and by her perfect personal cooperation with God's grace, the greatest of all God's creatures.

Our sources for knowledge of Mary are Scripture and tradition, and recall that Scripture itself sprang from the early oral tradition of the Church. If we reflect on the way tradition was built up, we can see why we know less about Mary than we would like to. Tradition accumulated information backwards. That is, the early Church realized that the central event in salvation history was the Passion, Death, and Resurrection of the Lord and this is what they first preached and gathered information on. Next they began to collect information about what Jesus said and did, his Public Life. Only then did they go back to the early life of Jesus where Mary played a central role, and by then many of the witnesses had died.

We see this reverse chronological quest of information reflected in Scripture. St. Paul, the first to set things down in writing, never even mentions Mary by name. He simply records that Jesus was born of a woman. Mark, the first Gospel written, also never mentions Mary by name. He provides no details of the birth of Jesus and starts his Gospel at the beginning of the Lord's Public

Life. In the whole of his Gospel Mary is mentioned only once and then only obliquely, when the crowds report to Jesus that his mother and brothers are outside looking for him.

In Matthew, the second Gospel written, we find an Infancy Narrative reporting the birth of Jesus. But Matthew's primary purpose is to show how Jesus fulfilled Old Testament prophecy. Since lineage was traced through one's biological or adoptive father, Matthew says little of Mary and centers his nativity account on Joseph who, as the foster father of Jesus, would determine the lineage of Jesus and link it to David.

By the time of Luke, the third Gospel, a notable change has taken place. Mary's greatness is now realized. The angel addresses Mary as full of grace, Elizabeth greets her as "the mother of my Lord," and Mary's inspired Magnificat foretells her future veneration as blessed. John, the last Gospel, is more a theology than a history, but it gives Mary a prominent role at the start of her Son's Public Life (Cana) and at the end (under the Cross).

The same gradual recognition of Mary took place in speculative theology. It was not until the fifth century that Mary's role was officially clarified. Nestorius, patriarch of Constantinople, claimed that Mary could not be called the Mother of God, as she was only the mother of his human nature. The Church condemned this belief as heresy in 431 and declared that Mary was truly the Mother of God, having given flesh to the Son of God in her womb.

To honor the newly defined dogma, the reigning pontiff erected a new basilica in Rome dedicated to Mary, the Mother of God, and decorated it with mosaics of Mary starting from the Annunciation and continuing on with the different scenes in which she played an important role in salvation history. One of the four major basilicas in Rome, St. Mary Major was for centuries the largest church in the world dedicated to Mary.

We can also trace the development of popular awareness of Mary's role through the history of art because art reflects theological belief. If you look at great paintings of a single scene over time such as the Annunciation, you will see marked changes. The earliest paintings portray Mary as a slight girl visited by a overwhelming figure of an angel who makes her tremble. Later as recognition of Mary's greatness grew, she is portrayed as a woman of substance visited by a rather subdued angel bowing humbly before her. And by Renaissance times, Mary is portrayed enthroned as a queen or empress, with the angel a mere courier or messenger kneeling at her feet. The same is true in architecture. Devotion to Mary is seen in the spread of churches dedicated to her throughout the world. Its full flowering occurred in the Middle Ages when great cathedrals like Chartres were routinely built in her honor and filled with priceless stained glass and statuary presenting a virtual encyclopedia of Christian teaching on Mary's vital role in salvation history [This insight into art was adapted from Augustine Grady, S.J., *Searching the Sunday Scriptures, Cycle A*, private publication, pp. 25-26].

Mary's role in life was to bring her Son, Jesus Christ, the eternal Word of God, into the world as one like us. Her role now is to bring us to her Son. As long as we recall Mary's role and her relationship to her Son, who as God far outstrips her in rank and importance, we need have no fear of paying her too much homage. Honoring the mother of a famous individual is a common way of honoring the individual himself. And no true man is ever threatened or offended by honor paid to the woman in his life, be it his mother, wife, or daughter.

Twelve Days of Christmas

I'm sure you have all heard the Christmas carol, "The Twelve Days of Christmas," with its haunting melody. Before the Christmas season comes to an end I thought you might be interested to learn something of its background and history. The carol dates back to the 16th century and its precise author is unknown. It has generally been assumed to consist of twelve nonsense verses built around a pretty melody. But in a fascinating article in *Our Sunday Visitor* (12/20/92), Fr. Gilhooley, a chaplain at St. Mary's College, informs us that the carol was written by the English Jesuits of the 16th century as a catechetical device and it is far from filled with nonsensical verses. The carol is akin to the apocalyptic literature of Scripture which used obscure symbols to hide its true meaning from the enemy in time of persecution. To understand the background that gave rise to the carol, let us look briefly at the history of Catholicism in 16th century England.

When Henry VIII was rebuffed by Rome in his bid to divorce Catherine of Aragon to marry Anne Boleyn, he declared himself head of the Church in England replacing the Pope and demanded that all swear an oath of allegiance to him as such. St. Thomas More, the Chancellor of the Realm, the equivalent of the Prime Minister today, refused the oath supporting the elimination of the Pope's authority and Henry had him publicly beheaded. Catholic convents and monasteries were closed and looted. The situation was worse under his son, Edward VI, and better during the short reign of Catherine's daughter, Mary Tudor. She was succeeded by her half-sister Elizabeth I, an ardent Protestant, the daughter of Anne Boleyn. The practice of the Catholic faith was banned. Priests were exiled and forbidden under pain of death from returning or performing the sacraments. It was a desperate, dreadful time.

But many priests risked their lives to come back and minister to the flock and many lay Catholics likewise risked their lives and fortunes to hear Mass and have their children baptized. Wealthy families built hiding places, called priests' holes, in their homes to hide priests in case their homes were raided by the secret police. The story is told of one priest who was almost caught in a surprise raid. He had just time to squeeze into his hole before the police broke in on the family. The police had obviously received a tip because they went right to the fireplace where the priest's hole was located. But try as they might, they couldn't find the entrance. Then in their frustration they ordered a fire to be lit to drive out the priest. When he didn't emerge, because to do so would subject the host family to prison or death, they ordered more logs on the fire. Eventually all were driven from the room by the intense heat and the police left in disgust. The family rushed to get the priest out of the hole but he was already dead, baked alive. He gave his life under cruel circumstances to save those whom he had come to serve. And he was only one of many.

With this as a background we can see the need for secrecy and deception. "The Twelve Days of Christmas" was written to educate the faithful in the doctrines of the faith and yet not be obvious to the persecutors. The numbers are simply a mnemonic to help Catholics remember some basic facts. Recall the words of the song. "On the twelfth day of Christmas, my true love gave to me: twelve lords a leaping, eleven pipers piping, ten ladies dancing, nine drummers drumming, eight maids a milking, seven swans a swimming, six geese a laying, five golden rings, four colly birds, three French hens, two turtle doves, and a partridge in a pear tree."

"The Twelve Days of Christmas" celebrates the official Christmas season which starts liturgically on Christmas Day and ends twelve days later on the Feast of the Epiphany. "My true love" refers to God, "me" is the individual Catholic. The "twelve lords a leaping" are the twelve basic beliefs of the Catholic Church as outlined in the Apostles Creed. The "eleven pipers piping" are the eleven Apostles who remained faithful after the treachery of Judas. The "ten ladies dancing" are the Ten Commandments. The "nine drummers drumming" are the nine choirs of angels which in those days of class distinction were thought important. The "eight maids a milking" are the Eight Beatitudes. The "seven swans a swimming" are the Seven Sacraments. The "six geese a laying" are the Six Commandments of the Church or the six days of creation. The "five golden rings" are the first five books of the Old Testament called the Torah which are generally considered the most sacred and important of all the Old Testament. The "four colly birds" are the Four Gospels. The "three French hens" are the Three Persons in God or the three gifts of the Wise Men. The "two turtle doves" represent the two natures in Jesus: human and divine or the two Testaments, Old and New. The "partridge" is the *piece de resistance*, Jesus himself, and the "pear tree" is the Cross.

The Magi

"Epiphany" is a Greek word meaning "revelation." What we celebrate today is the fact that God for the first time revealed himself to the Gentile or non-Jewish world in the person of the Magi. It often comes as a shock to Americans to learn that in many parts of the world Epiphany is more highly esteemed than Christmas. In the Eastern Churches, in much of western Europe, and most of Latin America, Epiphany is celebrated with greater joy than elsewhere in recognition of the fact that Jesus was not only born among us but chose to share the fullness of that revelation with the Gentile or non-Jewish world. Epiphany, or the Feast of the Three Kings, is also the time for giving gifts in many parts of the world, in imitation of the wise men.

In today's Gospel Matthew first celebrates the accomplishment and reward of the Magi. He goes to great pains to show how the Magi were yearning for God, searching nature and the heavens for signs; how they left everything, to follow a star in the hope it would lead them to God or his envoy; how they accepted the advice of foreigners willingly in pursuing their quest and even trusted the Scripture of another culture and creed. In short, he shows the Magi doing all they can, naturally speaking, to find God.

By way of contrast, Matthew then presents the behavior of his own people. He does this with a series of uncomplimentary comparisons to the wise men who with no history of revelation to help them made great efforts to find Jesus. First Matthew shows us King Herod, successor of David, shepherd of Israel. When Herod hears of the King of the Jews, he thinks not of adoration or leading his people to him. He thinks only of murder, to destroy the child and keep him from his throne. Next Matthew tells us of the priests and scribes, the religious leaders. They are well versed in Scripture and know where the Messiah will be born: Bethlehem, as predicted by the prophet Micah (5:2). But their hearts are cold and completely indifferent. They make no effort to find the child personally. Lastly, Matthew shows us the ordinary people. The city of Jerusalem, the capital of the country, home to the best and the brightest in the land, is also indifferent. Though Bethlehem is less than ten miles away, the people make no effort to go and look for the Messiah. Matthew's Infancy Narrative, then, while filled with joy over the faith of the Holy Family and the wise men, is nonetheless tinged with sadness due to the hostility and indifference of the chosen people themselves.

As an author, Matthew also uses this story which is a key opening scene in his Gospel to frame a key closing scene in the Gospel. Like a symphony that starts with a theme that is then repeated with different variations through the work until it explodes fully developed at the end, bringing the symphony together as a unity, Matthew uses a title to unite his Gospel and bring it together so that the opening story enlightens the ending and the end of the Gospel enriches the beginning.

One of the first titles Matthew records for Jesus at the start of the Gospel is "King of the Jews," and ironically it is given him by non-Jews, the Magi. As we saw in Matthew's earlier description, the Jewish world as represented by King Herod, the religious leaders, and the ordinary people of Jerusalem, put no stock in the title at all. At the end of the Gospel Matthew uses the same title tellingly again. It appears over the cross of Jesus: "Jesus of Nazareth, King of the Jews." And again, ironically, it is given to Jesus by a non-Jew, this time by Pilate, the Roman procurator. Matthew also employs a parallel cast of characters to show how his fellow countrymen have continued to deny Jesus his rightful title. Pilate asks Jesus, "Are you the King of the Jews?" (Mt 27:11). The chief priests and the elders accuse him, and the crowd rejects him in favor of Barabbas. When the soldiers mock Jesus, they say, "Hail, King of the Jews!" (Mt 27:29). After Jesus is crucified, the priests, scribes, and elders say, "He is the King of Israel; let him come down now from the cross, and we will believe in him" (Mt 27:42).

We can now better understand how carefully the beginning of Matthew's Gospel has been orchestrated to coordinate with the end of the Gospel. With the simple use of the title "King of the Jews," Matthew ties his Gospel together and shows the Jewish people how at all levels of society they failed at both the beginning and the end of the Public Life of Jesus to accept him as King and Messiah. The Magi who were never blessed with a history of revelation or God's personal intervention on their behalf, on the other hand, had no such difficulty and, irony of ironies, the pagan Roman procurator ends up trying to save Jesus from his very own people.

Matthew has taken a tough stand. He wrote at a time when Jewish religious leaders were persecuting the Church and excommunicating from the synagogues all who believed in Jesus. Still he writes more in disappointment than criticism. As a Jew himself, writing primarily for a Jewish audience, he wants more than anything else to lead his fellow countrymen, even shame them with the truth if necessary, into accepting Jesus as the Messiah. Hence he simply reminds his cherished people they have twice missed a chance to accept Jesus and he hopes they will reconsider in light of the whole Gospel message.

Jesus is Baptized

The event we commemorate in today's feast, the Baptism of the Lord, is an important event in the history of the Church and it is particularly esteemed in the Eastern Church. We know that it is an important event because the Baptism of the Lord is mentioned in all four Gospels whereas Christmas is mentioned only in two. Mark, the first Gospel written, begins with the Baptism of Jesus and does not even mention his birth. John, the last Gospel written, begins with a poetic prelude declaring Jesus co-eternal with the Father but then bypasses his birth and moves directly to his Baptism. Only Matthew and Luke mention the birth of Jesus but they also include his Baptism. So in the eyes of the evangelists who reflect the early Church, the Baptism of Jesus was clearly more important than Christmas. Perhaps we in the Church today miss the significance of the event because we fail to see the rich symbolism surrounding it.

In today's Gospel we are told the heavens opened, the Spirit descended, and a voice was heard. Each was rife with significance to members of the early Church, many of whom were Jewish. In Jewish cosmology in ancient times God was believed to inhabit the heavens, humankind the earth. Between the two was a barrier: the sky. At the time of Jesus the Jewish people felt forlorn. They had been conquered in swift succession by the Assyrians, the Babylonians, the Greeks, and the Romans. They felt as if God had forsaken them. For hundreds of years God had not sent a powerful king like David or a mighty military leader like Joshua. It was as if God had sealed off the heavens against them and remained impervious to their plight and pleas. Thus Isaiah pleaded, "Tear open the heavens and come down" (Is 63:19) and the Psalmist cried out, "Reach down from above and save me" (Ps 144:5-7). With the sky opening at the Baptism of the Lord, the early Christian community realized that God was once again intervening in human affairs, the long separation was ending, and a new era beginning.

Next we read that the Spirit of God descended like a dove and hovered above Jesus. The imagery is reminiscent of the story of creation in Genesis at the beginning of the Bible where we read that the Spirit of God hovered over the water before God began the process of creation. It suggests a new creation or re-creation of the world in which humankind will once again be close to God, closer to God than Adam and Eve were in the Garden of Eden, with Jesus as the new Adam giving the life of the Spirit to all who believe in him and making them true children of God.

Then a voice is heard from the heavens. This was most welcome because there had been no prophet in Israel for hundreds of years. God's voice had simply not been heard in the land. The heavens had remained painfully silent as in the time of Isaiah who complained to God, "How long can you oppress us with your silence?" (Is 64:11).

So against this background of popular awareness that the heavens had remained closed, the Spirit of God was absent from the land, and the voice of God had not been heard for generations, Matthew provides his account of the Baptism of Jesus with a powerful and dramatic introduction by simply noting the sky opened, the Spirit descended, and the voice of God was heard.

The proclamation from heaven, "This is my beloved son with whom I am well pleased," is clearly an approbation of Jesus and is a blend of two scriptural texts that help to explain who Jesus is and what he will do. The first comes from Psalm 2, "You are my son, this day I have begotten you," which speaks originally of the Messiah whom all were expecting. The second, "With whom I am well pleased," also translated as "On whom my favor rests," comes from Isaiah's description of the Suffering Servant who will please God by his total obedience (Is 42:1). The proclamation thus suggests early on in the Gospel that Jesus will be a suffering Messiah.

In his excellent book, *Illustrated Sunday Homilies*, Fr. Mark Link tells the story of Thor Heyerdahl, the author of *Kon-Tiki*, which aptly rounds out today's Gospel. In World War II while shooting rapids in a canoe, Thor Heyerdahl capsized and was drawn by the current to a lethal waterfall. As he was swept along, he wondered if his mother or perhaps his father was correct. His mother did not believe in an afterlife, his father did. He began to pray and suddenly realized the strength to break away from the current to safety. He emerged from his near death experience a totally different man. He was no longer an unbeliever but a believer.

Heyerdahl's experience is similar to what happens to us in Baptism. The person we are after Baptism is totally different from the person we were before Baptism. Before Baptism we were spiritually dead with no claim on God. After Baptism we are God's children, sharing in the life of the Spirit. Early Christians thought of Baptism as being grafted into the Body of Christ. If the branch doesn't become part of the tree and grow, it dies. So, too, with us. If we fail to live the life of Christ after Baptism, we will die spiritually. So let us pray today on the feast of the Baptism of the Lord, that we will truly cooperate with the grace of our Baptism and live as God's children, serving him and one another out of love and gratitude for the love God has freely bestowed on us.

Lamb of God

In today's Gospel John the Baptist catches sight of Jesus and ex-claims, "Behold the Lamb of God." What did he mean by this title and what did his Jewish audience understand by it? Five things come to mind.

1. *The Paschal Lamb.* John the Evangelist tells us that the scene occurred just before Passover (2:13). Passover was the big-gest and most important feast in the Jewish calendar. The timing would remind the Jewish audience of the paschal lamb, the lamb slain on the eve of the original Passover when the Jews were finally freed from their slavery in Egypt. The blood of the slain paschal lamb smeared on the door posts identified the Jewish families and protected their firstborn on the night when God's avenging angel struck down the firstborn in every Egyptian household (Ex 12:7-14). As a paschal lamb, Jesus would save his people from God's wrath and destruction. Ultimately he did this by shedding his own blood and laying down his life on the cross to save us from sin.

2. *The Temple Lambs.* Exodus 29:38 directs that every day for all time to come two one-year old lambs be sacrificed on the altar of atonement for sin, one in the morning and one in the evening. So long as the Temple stood this daily sacrifice was of-fered, even in time of hardship, hunger, famine, or siege. To many today this practice seems cruel and senseless. But we should recall in those days animals were raised for food and not as pets. A one-year old lamb was fully grown and was merely being diverted from the table to the altar. The Jewish people were simply trying to of-fer to God something very important to themselves. They lived in a subsistence economy. They needed sheep for food, wool, milk, and skins to hold wine. Surrendering a lamb to immolate to God was a considerable sacrifice for people who lived from hand to mouth. It showed they were willing to offer to God what was most

31

important and precious to themselves, their very sustenance. Since they could not offer their own lives in retribution for their sins, they offered the next best thing. As a Temple lamb, Jesus will offer his life in atonement for our sins.

3. *Servant or Prophet.* In Aramaic, the Semitic language which Jesus and John spoke, *talya* means both "lamb" and "servant." Prophets were commonly regarded as the servants of God. At least one also referred to himself specifically as a lamb. In speaking about the machinations hatched against him in his service of God, Jeremiah says, "I for my part was like a trustful lamb being led to the slaughter house, not knowing the schemes they were plotting against me" (Jr 11:19). Jesus is also clearly God's servant and prophet.

4. *The Messiah.* In the fourth of his Suffering Servant Songs referring to the Messiah, Isaiah speaks of God burdening the servant with the sins of the world and the servant bearing it all humbly and silently, like a lamb being led to slaughter (Is 53:6-7). In the imagery of Isaiah, John may well have seen Jesus as the Messiah who would save us by freely undergoing suffering.

5. *The Conquering Champion of God.* Quite different from the previous images of a gentle lamb is the lamb as conquering hero, an underdog who conquers a far superior foe. The image was used for Judah Maccabeus, a pious Jew who led his people in a successful revolt against the cruel Seleucid dynasty in 165 BC. Earlier the image was used of Samuel, David, and Solomon. We are perhaps most familiar with the image in Christian art where we see a young but fully mature lamb with horns standing before a banner and staff. The Book of Revelation uses the image twenty-nine times, a lamb of power, gentle but mighty.

There are thus many rich connotations for the title "Lamb of God": paschal lamb, Temple lamb, servant or prophet, Messiah, and conquering hero of God, all of which fit Jesus perfectly and illustrate different facets of his mission.

John the Baptist tells us twice that he did not at first recognize Jesus. But when he saw the Spirit descend and remain on Jesus, he then knew he was the promised one and proclaimed him as such to the Jewish people. What did the Jewish world understand by the Spirit? The Hebrew word for "spirit" is *ruach*, which also means "wind" or "breath." To the Hebrew mind, then, the Spirit was associated with power, like the force behind a mighty wind, a wind like that which swept through Paris in December 1999 and uprooted half the forest at Versailles, smashed priceless stained glass at Sainte Chapelle, and toppled the spires of Notre Dame. Spirit was also associated with life, for breath was the sign of life. The Spirit was also associated with illumination because the Spirit inspired wisdom and helped people to see the truth. And the Spirit was also associated with the presence of God, as when the Spirit of God was said to come upon a prophet or holy person. To the Jewish mind, then, the Spirit was a sign of God's coming into a person's life.

It is interesting to note that John saw the Spirit descend on Jesus and remain on him. This made Jesus unique and distinguished his Baptism from John's. John baptized with water, meaning his baptism was purely symbolic with no intrinsic efficacy of its own to restore a person to grace. Jesus, however, baptized with water and the Spirit. His Baptism is efficacious because through the merits of his Passion and Death he has the power to forgive sin, restore us to grace, and make us children of God once again.

Heathen Galilee

In this liturgical year we read mostly from Matthew and so it is good to understand something of his purpose and structure. Today's passage marks the beginning of the Public Life of Jesus. It recaps briefly Jesus' first spoken words, his selection of the first Apostles, and his first public miracles. And all three are introduced with a specific reference to Galilee. Why?

Galilee is the most northern of the three original provinces of Palestine. Stacked one on top of the other like building blocks, the three provinces from north to south were Galilee, Samaria, and Judah, with Jerusalem, the capital, located in the southernmost province of Judah. The name "Galilee" comes from *Galil*, meaning "encircled," because the province was completely surrounded by pagans and heretics. To the west was Phoenicia; to the north and east, Syria; and to the south, Samaria. At the time of Jesus Samaria was inhabited by the Samaritans whom the Jews regarded as half-breeds and heretics for having intermarried with pagans and adjusted to their ways. Surrounded by pagan cultures in the north, the Galileans, too, were suspected of succumbing to pagan influences. Cut off from easy access to Jerusalem and the Temple by hostile Samaritan neighbors in the south, they were criticized for their oftentimes sporadic fulfillment of religious duties. To the pious people in the environs of the Temple, they were seen as living in darkness and a spiritual void.

Using this common perception, Matthew inaugurates his account of the Lord's Public Life by proclaiming that Jesus has come as a light amid darkness by starting his preaching in Galilee. In so doing Matthew also suggests that Jesus is fulfilling the prophecy of Isaiah from the first reading and repeated in the Gospel. Napthali and Zebulun were both within the borders of Galilee, as was the Sea of Galilee itself. The citation from Isaiah comes from the section called the Book of Emmanuel in which Isaiah foretells that God will send someone special to lead his people, someone who would be called Wonder Counselor, Mighty God, Prince of Peace (Is 9:5-6).

The occasion for Jesus beginning his Public Life in Matthew's Gospel is the arrest of John the Baptist. With John in prison, his voice silenced, Jesus picks up his mantle and continues his work. He takes up John's theme of calling for repentance and proclaims the fact that the kingdom of God is at hand. But Jesus gives new meaning and urgency to John's words. When John announced the kingdom of God was at hand, he meant it was simply near. When Jesus says the kingdom of God is at hand, he means it has actually dawned. In his person, words, and saving acts, Jesus truly issues in the kingdom of God, makes it present on earth, and invites all to participate and share in God's love. Hence the urgency and need for repentance lest people miss the uniqueness of the moment, the priceless opportunity that was finally at hand now that God's Son was physically present among them.

Matthew's introduction to the Public Life is very sketchy, however. He tells us that Jesus preached, using the word *kerussein*, which refers to proclaiming the king's word with authority. But he does not at this point tell of what Jesus preached. He tells us Jesus called Peter, Andrew, James, and John as Apostles, but he gives us no specifics regarding what their mission entailed. He tells us that Jesus taught in the synagogues, but nothing of what he taught. He tells us Jesus cured people of many diseases but he does not tell us what the diseases were. Matthew is deliberately being elliptical at this point in his Gospel in order to build up suspense. He wants his readers to ask themselves important questions. Who is this Jesus who speaks with such authority, summons disciples who leave everything to follow him, and cures the sick of every kind of illness? What is the message he brings, what is the reason for his coming? Matthew will begin to answer these questions in the beginning of his next chapter which we will read starting with next Sunday. It is called the Sermon on the Mount and it begins with the Beatitudes which contain the kernel of Jesus' teaching and approach to life.

The prophecy that Matthew incorporates into today's Gospel is from First Isaiah. First Isaiah urged the Jewish people to place their faith in Yahweh and not in foreign alliances for peace and prosperity. From a religious point of view he feared that any commitment to a foreign power would contaminate the purity of their monotheistic belief in Yahweh and signal a diminution of their confidence in his divine providence. From a practical viewpoint he realized the larger nations might simply absorb them into their borders. The northern kingdom of Israel did not heed Isaiah's advice and was soon overwhelmed by Assyria. Its ten tribes were exiled to various parts of the Assyrian Empire. There they lost their faith and national identity as Isaiah feared and are referred to in history as the ten lost tribes of Israel.

Isaiah intensified his efforts on behalf of Judah with its two remaining tribes in the south. In chapters 6-9, called the Book of Emmanuel, from which the first reading is taken, Isaiah tells of a ruler whom God will send to save his people. In today's reading Isaiah speaks of darkness, distress, and gloom; yokes, rods, burdens, and taskmasters — all signs of oppression brought on the northern kingdom by its refusal to trust in God. Here Isaiah assures the people that God has the power to reverse it if they simply trust in him again.

Sermon on the Mount (Beatitudes)

Up until this point in his Gospel Matthew has told us that Jesus went about teaching and preaching and people were spellbound by what he had to say. But aside from, "Repent and reform your lives," he has not told us specifically what Jesus taught. Having built up our suspense and curiosity, he now begins to unfold a considerable body of his thought, blending the teaching of Jesus into a single sermon, now known as the Sermon on the Mount. This sermon fills the next three chapters of Matthew's Gospel and will carry us through five more Sundays of Gospel readings.

In his Gospel Matthew is anxious to show his Jewish audience that Jesus is like Moses who was the greatest teacher, leader, and law giver of the Old Testament. Since Moses received his revelation from God on Mount Sinai and a mountain was typically the place of revelation, Matthew is careful to tell us Jesus too went up the mountainside before he revealed his teaching to his disciples. Like all rabbis, Moses sat when he taught, a position of authority in the Jewish world, much as a judge even today sits at the bench when deciding cases and the Pope defines dogma "ex cathedra," that is, seated on the chair of St. Peter.

In Matthew, Jesus begins his long-awaited teaching with the Beatitudes, the most frequently quoted words of Jesus after the Our Father. The Beatitudes represent the kernel or outline of Jesus' teaching. Moses had emphasized the contractual arrangements of the Old Testament covenant with God which stressed what the people had to do for God. This unwittingly led to a distortion of the role of external observance of the law, outward compliance with Temple rituals, and the people's own importance in the process. Jesus takes another tack. He stresses God's initiative and humankind's unworthiness. It is not a matter of tit for tat or a *quid pro quo*, of our obeying a law and God rewarding us for doing so.

Our salvation is a gift from God who loves us first and foremost, even the most wretched. So rather than present a host of prescriptions and injunctions, or a list of do's and don'ts as outlined in the Mosaic Law, Jesus presents a series of attitudes calling for an inner conversion and radical transformation of life, an emptying of self and a total commitment to God and his will for us and for the world. From the very outset, Jesus makes it clear that God's ways are not our ways. The ancient Jewish world believed that prosperity and well-being were a sign of God's predilection; their absence, a mark of divine disfavor. Jesus explodes that myth. The kingdom of God, he announces, is not for the rich or blissful but for the sorrowing and poor in spirit. What the world admires, God despises. God judges by different standards and Jesus now makes clear what those standards are.

In choosing beatitudes to encapsulate his teaching, Jesus was making use of a pedagogical device common to the Old Testament, particularly the Psalms and Wisdom literature. There are over eighty beatitudes in the Old Testament. In them, the word "blessed" means honored, esteemed, or approved by God. It is used at the beginning of a beatitude to describe a type of conduct or disposition of soul that elicits God's approbation. It is generally followed immediately by an expression in the passive voice (be filled, be consoled), called the theological or divine passive because it is a way that devout Jews, out of reverence, regularly employed to avoid using God's name. The clear implication is always, however, that the blessing will come from God.

Notice the spiritual tone and quality of the characteristics singled out in those destined for God's blessing in Matthew's Beatitudes. It is decidedly different in character from the attributes enumerated in Luke's version where the physical side of the same qualities seem to dominate. Whereas Matthew is careful to qualify the poor *in spirit* and those who hunger *for justice*, for instance, Luke speaks simply of the poor, the hungry, the weeping, the persecuted, reflecting his special love and concern for the *anawim* who were materially the poorest of the poor, without rights or anyone to stand up for them. Returning to Matthew's version, we see:

1. Blest are the poor in spirit: those who realize their utter need of God and the poverty of life without him.
2. Blest are those who mourn: those who grieve over the state of the world, their sins, and the sins of others.
3. Blest are the meek and lowly: those who realize their place before God and don't try to impose their will on him. The land they are promised is the kingdom of heaven.
4. Blest are those who hunger and thirst for righteousness: those who yearn for God's way of doing things to become the norm of human conduct and act accordingly.
5. Blest are the merciful: those who forgive as God forgives and who do not hold grudges or seek revenge.
6. Blest are the clean of heart: those who act from the purest motives of love for God alone and single-heartedly seek to do his will.
7. Blest are the peacemakers: those who are reconciled with God, themselves, and others and help others to enjoy the same peace.
8. Blest are the persecuted for the sake of Jesus: those who suffer or are demeaned for their beliefs and observance of God's laws. Their reward will be great in heaven.

Salt of the Earth

William Barclay has a series of books on both the Old and New Testaments that offers wonderful insights and background materials for understanding Scripture. His first volume on the Gospel of Matthew is particularly helpful for today's passage. In today's Gospel Jesus uses three simple but powerful metaphors of what he expects of his followers. His disciples should be like salt, light, and a city set upon a hilltop. Let us examine each in turn.

At the time of Jesus the Romans had a saying, *"Nihil utilius est sole et sale."* Nothing is more useful than the sun and salt. The sun's importance is obvious. Without the light and warmth of the sun, human life could not exist upon this planet. But why salt? The modern world often forgets three of its essential properties. (1) Salt is an antiseptic. It kills bacteria. Women in ancient times cleaned chicken with rock salt to prevent salmonella. Before iodine it was the only thing available to clean a wound. Rubbing salt in a wound hurt, but it prevented infection. So salt was important as a purifier, a preventer of diseases. (2) Salt is a preserver. Before refrigeration the only way to preserve meat or fish was to salt or smoke them. Salt draws the moisture out and decomposition cannot take place without moisture. Hence salt was vital as a preserver. (3) Salt is an enhancer. It brings out flavor on the stove and on the table. Without substitutes or others herbs and spices, food is generally insipid, meals bland, as anyone on a salt-free diet knows. Salt is essential to add zest to life and cooking.

Today we have refined salt. In those days salt was gotten from mines where it was mixed with other minerals and impurities or it was obtained from beds of dried sea water which also contained sand and other residue. To cope with the impurities, people placed the salt in a porous pouch and dropped pouch and all into the stew or soup to simmer. The salt would dissolve and permeate the food while the impurities would remain trapped in the pouch. Eventually when the salt was all used up and only the impurities left, it would have to be thrown out. It was useless. Jesus invites us to be like salt: purifiers, cleansers, preservers, people who add zest to life by giving it God's flavor.

Jesus also calls us to be a light. Homes in ancient Palestine generally consisted of one room with no windows and only a door. When the door was closed, the house would be pitch black. Light came from a small oil lamp. If the lamp were placed low, anyone standing in front of it would block the light. So it was placed on a stand or ledge above everyone's head so all could see it and profit from it. Without a lamp or oil to fill it, people had no choice but to sleep. There could be no guests, activities, or socializing without light. Christians should be like a light, facilitating communications among families and neighbors and contributing to the joys of life. Light was also used in lanterns to guide travelers at night and keep them from mishap. As Christians we should also be lights in leading people to God and away from evil. Light was also used to warn people of danger, much as flares are used today. Torches were commonly set up in port channels to keep ships at night away from shoals. As Christians we should strive to help others steer a clear course, away from danger and towards our loving Father.

Lastly, Jesus asks us to be like a city on a hilltop. Cities were usually built on high ground so they could more easily be defended. They were also placed there, however, so they could be seen. As centers of commerce, they wanted to attract traders and travelers. With few maps, poor roads, and no directional sign posts, an elevated city could more easily be found. As Christians, we should be like an elevated city, a beacon drawing others into our community of faith.

Besides the strong positive connotations enumerated so far for the three metaphors of salt, light, and a hilltop city, the first two images also offer the Christian some interesting caveats. We are called to be salt. But salt, we should always remember, is never desired for itself. Too much salt ruins the taste of food. As Christians we should simply be enhancers, enabling people to come to God but never getting in the way or interfering. We are called to be a light. But a light is never meant to be looked at for itself. It could be blinding. A light is intended to illuminate the surroundings and allow other objects to be seen. As Christians we are to brighten this world by our lives so others can see the love of God at work in us and come to share in the fullness of that love too.

In the first reading, Isaiah shows he knows the true meaning of light which Jesus calls for in today's Gospel. Writing to the exiles on their return home to Jerusalem from the Babylonian captivity, Isaiah calls on them to be an authentic light, not preoccupied with the externals of the law but careful to fulfill the heart of the law, which is love of God and neighbor, by feeding the hungry, clothing the naked, sheltering the homeless. St. Paul, in the second reading, also demonstrates full appreciation of today's Gospel message. He makes no special claims for himself but simply preaches the message of Jesus Christ and him crucified. His ministry was to bring people to God and then step humbly and completely out of the way.

As Christians, let us remember the true sense in which we are to be salt, light, and a hilltop city.

Not to Abolish the Law, but to Fulfill It

Jeremiah promised the days would come when God would place his law within the hearts of his people, a time when they would no longer need to read it on stone tablets for it would be written in their hearts (Jr 31:33). In today's Gospel as Jesus continues the Sermon on the Mount we began two weeks ago, he delivers on that promise by showing how his teaching differs from the Mosaic Law and how it does not abolish the law but fulfills it.

To see how Jesus' teaching fulfills the Mosaic Law, we should recall how the law evolved. When Moses led the Jewish people out of Egypt into the desert where God forged them together as a nation for the first time, they reflected the morality of their times and surroundings. It was a time when might made right and people felt free to enslave others, as the Egyptians did the Jews; to manhandle or kill anyone who opposed them; to treat workers like cattle and women like chattel; to rob, rape, pillage, and plunder. Everyone was simply a law to himself.

Into this moral morass God sent Moses with the Ten Commandments to forge the beginning of a new moral sense or code of decency. The Ten Commandments represented the basics or bare minimum of what people had to do to behave humanly and live as God's children. But basic or minimal as they were, they still proved difficult for humankind to accept and it took generations for them to become the norm. In the interim Moses formulated other laws to help the people keep the Ten Commandments. "An eye for an eye, a tooth for a tooth," which sounds barbaric by today's standards, was actually added to introduce a note of reason and proportionality by curbing the excessive retaliation and retribution that prevailed at the time. God, if you will, intended the Ten Commandments as the first steps towards morality, to help the people form the basics from which they could grow.

Finally, God sends his Son. By the time of the Sermon on the Mount, Jesus can assume people know they cannot kill or steal or live their lives accordingly. So he is free to invite them to a new and higher form of morality, the fullness of the law, where people are encouraged to go beyond the minimum of external observance and to internalize the law as Jeremiah foresaw. In this Jesus moves contrary to organized religion at the time. The scribes and Pharisees worked from the principle of the law outward to every conceivable application and possibility, multiplying precepts, increasing obligations, exaggerating minutiae, and making knowledge of the law more difficult and its fulfillment increasingly burdensome. Jesus, by way of contrast, worked from the principle of the law inward, to the attitude or frame of mind that would bring about compliance with the law and lead to its perfect fulfillment. The approach Jesus will introduce simplifies the law and makes it easier to comprehend. But it also makes it far more challenging.

Accordingly, Jesus tells his followers it is not only wrong to kill, it is wrong to grow angry because anger can lead to violence and bloodshed. If we control our inner feelings and not allow anger to swell up in us, we will never resort to violence and murder. Cut the sin off at its root and it can never develop. We will maintain a proper regard for our fellow men and women. And here it is interesting to note that Jesus uses the word *orge* which means "an inveterate anger which one nurses and broods over and stokes," not *thumos* which means "an emotional annoyance which quickly fades." The Ten Commandments tell us it is wrong to commit adultery. With this type of sin, Jewish rabbis then, as Catholic theologians now, frequently legislated in terms of how far a person might go before sinning. Jesus to the contrary nips it in the bud. He tells his disciples not even to think of it, thereby introducing a more demanding ethic requiring control over both mind and heart. The law permitted an oath to verify one's veracity. Jesus condemns the practice of placing demands on God to act as a witness on one's behalf and tells his followers plainly they must always speak the truth, not merely when under oath. In sum, rather than abolish the law, Jesus calls for a higher form of law and behavior, one that goes far beyond external observance to an interior conversion so that the rationale and motivation behind the law will become the guiding force behind all our actions and our very way of life. This motivation and rationale he will formalize later in the Sermon on the Mount when he sums up the whole law in two precepts: love of God and love of neighbor.

Before closing, two points need clarification. One, when Jesus speaks of cutting off one's hand or plucking out one's eye, he is using Semitic exaggeration and does not intend to be taken literally. His aim here is to alter our innermost attitudes, not our physical appearance. Two, Moses permitted divorce for lewd conduct (Dt 24:1). Conservative rabbis took that to mean adultery; liberals, anything offensive to the husband. The early Church understood two things in Jesus' use of the term: (1) an incestuous union between two people closely related by blood, such as siblings, that would render any marriage illegal and therefore null and void; and (2) a nefarious practice in ancient times wherein the guardian of an orphaned heiress, frequently her uncle, would use his position to force her to marry him so he could gain full control of her estate. It was the worst combination of the dirty old man and the greedy old man, and the lack of freedom on the part of the girl would strike down any such union as null and void.

Love Your Enemy

Today's Gospel marks the fourth Sunday in a row we continue with the Sermon on the Mount in which Jesus lays out his teaching and shows how it differs from that of Moses. In Exodus 21:24 Moses called for "an eye for an eye, a tooth for a tooth." It seems harsh to us today but we should realize that it was meant to moderate excessive forms of retaliation. At the time of Moses it was not uncommon for an injured party to respond by taking the life or lives of anyone remotely involved in the injury, such as the wife, children, and tribesmen of the offender. Vestiges of this practice remain even today among some peoples. In the Balkans warring factions have wiped out whole towns and villages for offenses committed hundreds of years ago. What Moses was trying to do was to rein in this type of outrageous behavior by introducing a note of proportionality or reason. But the people, long used to vengeance and venting their wrath, found it difficult to accept, and even more difficult to implement. In today's Gospel Jesus pushes Moses' ethic a giant step further with two new directives.

1. "Offer no resistance to injury." It is a difficult teaching, a demanding ethic. It tells us we must act lovingly and not respond in kind to those who do evil. As Christians, we can never reduce ourselves to the level of those who perpetrate evil against us. Yet how is this possible? How can we show love for those who have no love for us, turn the other cheek when they have struck us, walk the extra mile, hand over our coat? In telling us to be perfect like our heavenly Father, Jesus suggests we simply recall how often we try our heavenly Father's patience, how often we sin or fail, and come back again and again for forgiveness. If God forgives us our sins and we want to return to his love, should we not also be willing to forgive others?

Still the advice at a strictly human level seems suicidal, leaving us without defense or protection. So let us be clear about what love means. Love means never stooping to evil, never being spiteful or harmful to one who has offended or harmed us, never seeking simply to hurt or repay the harm. Love means wishing the other only well and a speedy return to God's grace. Love does not mean, however, exposing oneself to harm by remaining in an abusive situation. Anyone who is a victim of abuse should extricate himself or herself from harm, seek restriction on the other's use of force, and try to find them help if possible. Similarly, the Gospel does not encourage us to stand by idly while someone else is maltreated. Love calls for us to defend the injured party while seeking ways to help the offender change his ways or be restrained. Confronted with someone who is addicted to alcohol, drugs, or gambling, for example, love doesn't call us to accept and thus abet the person's problem but to insure the person gets help.

2. "Love your enemies." Another seemingly impossible injunction. But remember Jews at the time regarded all non-Jews as enemies for failing to acknowledge the one, true God. Their distinction between friend and foe hinged almost entirely on bonds of family, blood, race, and religion. The word "enemy" was by no means limited to those who had personally offended them. In adding a universal note to the scope of love required of his disciples, Jesus clearly challenged his early Jewish followers, many of whom found it difficult to welcome Gentiles into the early Church.

Knowing that "enemy" was synonymous with "Gentile" softened the command of love of enemy for the non-Jewish world in some ways but the addition of "pray for your persecutors" put them quickly back on the hook. Jesus makes it clear we are to love and wish the best even for those who do us mortal harm. Taken together, the two commands seem totally unrealistic, forcing the human heart to ask how it can possibly be done.

Let's look at an example. Suppose you had an only child who was run down and killed by a drunk driver. Would you be able to forgive the driver, plead with the court for clemency on his behalf, feel real warmth and concern for his future well being? Now suppose it's your child who runs down and kills someone else's child while legally under the influence. Wouldn't you want the aggrieved family to forgive your child and intercede with the court for clemency so his or her life would not be ruined? When we love the culprit, we can see good in him and reason to forgive. Jesus asks us to love others. If we truly loved them, perhaps we would more readily forgive.

An old priest once told me of being called to the hospital late at night during Prohibition. A gangster had been mortally wounded in an attempted rub out. A Catholic by birth, the dying man had never practiced his religion. Before giving absolution, the priest asked if he were sorry for all his sins. The man said yes. The priest next asked if he forgave his assailant. The man replied no. If he lived, he would kill him. The priest then told him he couldn't absolve him because God requires us to forgive others as a condition for his forgiving us. The man then asked if God would forgive him all his sins if he forgave the one who shot him? The priest replied yes. The man then asked to see his lieutenant who was standing outside. The man entered. The dying man told him that the plans were changed and he wanted him to swear on the priest's Bible that there would be no revenge when he died. The man was startled but agreed to his dying friend's request and the priest gave him general absolution. He died the next day in God's love because he had the courage to take God at his word and forgive his enemies, even the man who shot him.

You Cannot Serve God and Mammon

Today's Gospel is a continuation of the Sermon on the Mount with its systematic unfolding and development of the central core of Jesus' teachings. This particular section is aptly summed up in its introductory and concluding remarks: "No one can serve two masters," and "Seek first the kingdom of God." For the Gospel passage bears on priorities and the need to keep them straight. If God and his law are first among our priorities, everything else will fall into place. If they are not, our lives will be all out of kilter, courting disaster. Among the things most likely to confuse our hierarchy of values Jesus singles out money which humankind frequently craves for the power, security, and comfort it affords them. If money, either for itself or for any of the things it makes humanly possible, becomes uppermost in our minds or hearts, other important aspects of our lives suffer. When God does not come first, our lives can unwind.

Some commentators see in Jesus' opening remark, "No one can serve two masters," a recasting of the central theme of the Torah, "You shall love the Lord, your God, with your whole heart, your whole soul, and your whole strength." (Dt 6:5). It is simply another way of saying we must give wholehearted, undivided service and devotion to the Lord. Other commentators see the contending masters for human attention as the kingdom of God and the spirit of the world, both diametrically opposed one to the other, and both vying to win as many adherents to its side as possible, ideally to the full exclusion of the other. It is a life and death struggle on whose outcome depends the salvation of each and every one of us.

In today's passage the prose invades the realm of poetry, revealing Jesus once again as a master, mesmerizing communicator. Jesus uses two extraordinary images to encourage trust in his almighty Father. One is of the birds in the sky who neither sow nor reap but are fed by their heavenly Father; the other is of the lilies of the field who neither spin nor sew but are clothed more splendidly than Solomon. We are worth more than many sparrows or any plant that withers and ends as kindling for the fire, Jesus assures us, and we should have a corresponding faith in God.

The translation of the word "lily" is often called into question. The Aramaic word means "wild flower," of which lilies are only one variety. The Greek word, *krina*, used in the original translation, means "lily" but it is a species of lily found in the woodlands and not in the fields. Some commentators, therefore, lean to "wild flowers" as the more appropriate translation and feel it is the more suitable image. Throughout the early part of the year the fields of Galilee are filled with a glorious array of different wild flowers that color the landscape and command attention, chief among them being anemones and poppies.

One perceptive commentator whom I unfortunately cannot recall suggests the use of metaphor in the selection of the images. In Aramaic, a language related to Hebrew that was commonly spoken in the time of Jesus, the word for "bird" is masculine and the word for "wild flower" or "lily" is feminine. The tasks spared the birds in today's Gospel were typically men's jobs: sowing and reaping, providing food for the family. The tasks eluding the flowers of the field were specifically women's chores: spinning and sewing, outfitting the family with clothes. The use of the double image directs both men and women in their specific areas of responsibility not to be overwhelmed with the concerns of this life or come to think of themselves as indispensable. Try as they might, succeed as they might, they cannot add a moment to their life span.

Two caveats should also be included with this reflection. While Jesus is telling us not to be anxious, he is not urging us to be passive. "Let tomorrow take care of itself," does not mean putting off for tomorrow what should be done today. It does not mean "*manana*," in the unfair and unfortunate, though frequently common, stereotyping of Latin American ways. Nor is it the equivalent of the teenager's "Later," mumbled in response to a request to wash the dishes or take out the garbage. If our priorities are correct, seeking first the kingdom of God means fulfilling responsibilities and taking care of all entrusted to us to the best of our ability, while always trusting in God above all else to provide whatever is essential.

The second caveat is to be aware of the audience Jesus was addressing. The setting for the Sermon on the Mount is Galilee and Galilee was geographically the best endowed and most productive part of Palestine. Though most people in those days had to work hard for a living, the people of Galilee by and large were comparatively well off. The region produced enough food so that people generally did not go hungry and the climate was sufficiently mild so shelter was not a pressing problem. Jesus here is not speaking to an audience that had to worry about where the next meal was coming from or if indeed they would have anything at all to eat. Jesus is essentially telling an audience that was reasonably provided for not to be overly concerned with the material things in life, not to be preoccupied with amassing more and more possessions, but to put God first and seek the truly important things in life.

Those driven to get ahead financially or career-wise encounter many obstacles to home life: long hours, working weekends, extended trips. They do all of this to get ahead financially or professionally while spouse and children are deprived of an important, irreplaceable presence. The drive for profit can also affect our streams and air as business spews waste into air and rivers. Such decisions, while corporate, are generally made by individuals who can see no farther than the bottom line.

Not Everyone Who Says, "Lord, Lord"

Today's Gospel ends the Sermon on the Mount which we began to read from six Sundays ago. It started on the Fourth Sunday of the Year with the Beatitudes from Matthew, chapter 5. There Jesus proposed a new and revolutionary set of values by which he expected his followers to lead their lives. The Sermon continues to its high point in Matthew 6:10 where Jesus teaches us to pray and recites for us the perfect prayer, the Our Father. It is the central and single most important teaching in the Sermon on the Mount. Jesus then devotes the rest of the Sermon on the Mount to a series of teachings that further develop the themes of the Lord's Prayer, with an explanation for most of the key verses, but presented in an ancient Semitic style of reverse order. With that in mind, let us recall the Our Father in reverse order.

1. "Lead us not into temptation." When tempted by Satan in the desert, Jesus replied he would serve God alone (Mt 4:10). Last week we read (Mt 6:24), "No one can serve two masters." Both of these passages serve as images to explain the last invocation of the Our Father. In praying to be kept from temptation, we pray not to be misled by false values, that like Jesus we will always realize that we are to serve God alone. Matthew (6:33) further reinforces the idea by concluding the passage with "Seek first the kingdom of God."

2. "Forgive us our trespasses as we forgive those who trespass against us." In Matthew 7:1 Jesus tells us in a slightly different format, "Do not judge, and you will not be judged; because the judgments you give are the judgments you will get, and the amount you measure out is the amount you will be given." He concludes with a further vivid image of spotting a speck in our brother's eye while being unaware of a plank in our own.

3. "Give us this day our daily bread." In Matthew 7:9 Jesus

"I am the Way, the Truth, and the Life"

The evangelists wrote the Gospels to report what Jesus said and did in his lifetime and to convey it to the early Church in a way they could understand and appreciate. So the needs of the early Church in some ways shaped the Gospels themselves. Today's Gospel helps to illustrate this point. Let us start with the historical narrative, the report of what happened, and then see how the scriptural reporting took shape.

In today's Gospel, set at the Last Supper, the night before he died, Jesus tells his disciples, "I am going to prepare a place for you." "Going to prepare" does not mean "will prepare." It means departing *in order* to prepare. It is the same verb John uses to convey Jesus' movement toward his passion and death. The verse implies, therefore, that Jesus is going to his passion and death in order to prepare a place for us.

The mention of departure stirs up anxiety in the Apostles. When Thomas says to him, "Master, we do not know where you are going; how can we know the way?" Jesus answers enigmatically with, "I am the Way, the Truth, and the Life." All three terms have their roots in Old Testament history.

1. *The Way.* In Deuteronomy God tells Moses, "You must walk in the way I have commanded you." Moses in turn tells the people, "You must not stray from the ways of the Lord." Isaiah points out to the people, "This is the way of the Lord. Walk in it." And the psalmist prays, "Teach me your ways, O Lord." Here Jesus deliberately applies the concept to himself. In doing so, he is not referring to a geographical path or route one must follow. The way to the Father is not to walk where Jesus walked, but to live as Jesus lived, to model our life and attitudes on him because he is the fullest, most perfect expression of God's love. It can best be expressed in terms of an analogy. Suppose you come to a strange town and

ask for directions. You might get a series of lefts and rights, which would overwhelm you and leave you hopelessly lost. Or you might get someone who would show you the way so you couldn't get lost. Jesus didn't simply give us a series of directives, he showed us the way by going before us.

2. *The Truth*. The psalmist says, "Teach me your ways, so I may walk in your truth," and later, "I have chosen the way of truth." Truth is that which conforms to reality. As human beings, we are all creatures of God. By living his human life perfectly, subjecting himself to God the Father in all things, Jesus is the embodiment of truth: what it is to be truly human. By way of analogy, many have told us the truth and tried to explain what moral goodness is, but no one except Jesus has embodied it. Yet moral truth cannot be conveyed solely in words. No one believes someone whose actions belie his words; as, for example, a crook preaching honesty. Moral truth is best conveyed by example and Jesus has given us the perfect example.

3. *The Life*. When the psalmist pleads, "Show me the path to life," he is not seeking knowledge for itself but to make life worth living, to give it a purpose. In showing us through his life and example how to live as truly God's children, Jesus opens for us the way to heaven and eternal life. Through the merits of his upcoming passion and death, he will gain access for us to life with him and his Father that will never end.

Jesus also tells Philip, "Whoever has seen me has seen the Father." This was shocking. The Jews believed no one could see the face of God and live. The great patriarchs, Abraham, Isaac, and Jacob, saw only God's messengers, the angels, never God himself. Here Jesus makes a claim that other important religious leaders never dared make. Jesus is truly the Son of God, the love of God made manifest on earth.

To conclude the first point about the historical narrative, the disciples were anxious because Jesus was leaving. Jesus' most likely historical reply suggested they live their lives as he lived his and they too would have God's life in them and would one day also go to the Father and be with him forever.

Now let us turn to the second point: how and why given events were recorded and communicated to the early Church. The early Church was much like the Apostles in today's Gospel. Jesus had in fact left and ascended into heaven. They felt alone and anxious. Many were simply waiting for the Second Coming, sitting idly by. So John in today's Gospel in effect directs Jesus' words at them. The words and incident were remembered, repeated, and recorded precisely because this historical incident in Jesus' life closely paralleled the conditions in John's community. John uses the story to remind his peers that Jesus did not intend them to sit helplessly and hopelessly by waiting for his return. In the account John has Jesus tell all future followers, not just the Apostles, how to live in his absence. We are to follow his way, model our lives on his, and in that way bring God's presence and reign into the world. By continuing his work on earth, in imitation of him, we will build up his kingdom on earth and prepare ourselves for a place in the kingdom of heaven. Moreover, he promises that the works we do in his name will be far greater than his. Greater here does not mean better, but more extensive, more spread out in space and time through the members of his body, but similarly effective if done in union with him.

John likewise directs Jesus' historical words to Philip to the early Church. "Have I been with you for so long a time and you still do not know me?" Here he is referring to his presence in the Church through the sacraments, a presence that is just as real as when he walked the earth. A presence that likewise demands a response.

The Paraclete

Today's Gospel comes from the Last Supper, the night before Jesus died, just before they all left the Upper Room to go the garden of Gethsemane to pray. The Apostles are dispirited at the thought of Jesus leaving them, so he tries to console them. Let us look at two parts of the text.

First, Jesus promises to send another Paraclete. "Paraclete" is a difficult word to translate and so it has come down to us simply transliterated from the Greek into English. In brief, "Paraclete" is the original Greek word expressed in English. Literally it means "one called in to help." But it can have many distinct meanings and connotations, depending on the circumstances in which it is used. I'll mention five, all of which are germane to the Holy Spirit.

1. *Advocate.* "Paraclete" can correctly be translated as "advocate" in cases where one is called in to defend or speak up for another, such as a defense attorney or character witness. In such cases the person is called in to be an advocate for the other.

2. *Healer.* "Paraclete" can correctly be translated as "healer" if one is called in at a time of sickness, disease or plague to provide medical attention or consultation in search of a cure. "Paraclete" in such cases would indicate "a healer or physician."

3. *Helper.* If one is called in to lend a hand and give assistance in time of trouble or need, "Paraclete" can correctly be defined as "a helper, aide, or assistant."

4. *Counselor.* If one is called in time of confusion or crisis for advice on what to do or how to proceed, the one summoned is expected to function as a counselor.

5. *Comforter.* The word does not mean "a shoulder to cry on" as we often think of it today. It means "comforter" in the sense of its Latin root, *cum forte*, "one called in to give strength, determination, or courage." It is aptly illustrated by a general talking to

his troops before battle, or a coach giving a pep talk to his team before the big game, or a teacher offering words of wisdom and encouragement to pupils before a standardized test like the Regents exams or SATs.

The Holy Spirit embodies all of the above. He is our Advocate, Healer, Helper, Counselor, and Comforter. If pressed to sum them all up in one word, I would choose Enabler. The Spirit, whom Jesus will send after his departure at the Ascension, is the one who will enable us to follow after Jesus and lead a truly Christian life.

Jesus specifically mentions *another* Paraclete. With this Jesus simply reminds us that he too was a Paraclete in his own life: an advocate, healer, helper, counselor, comforter / strengthener, enabler in the Christian life. To console his Apostles on his departure in today's Gospel he promises to send the Holy Spirit, the third Person of the Blessed Trinity to replace him. The role of the Holy Spirit, the Paraclete, then, is to replace Jesus, to take over his role as the initial Enabler after Jesus ascends to the Father. God shows his great love for us by continuing his saving presence among us.

The second point worth noting is that Jesus also promises not to leave his disciples orphans. In ancient times, when a religious leader died, his followers regarded themselves as orphans because they were bereft of their spiritual leader, guide, and father. Even in the secular world, when Socrates died, Plato referred to the pupils he left behind as orphans. By sending the Spirit, the Enabler, to replace himself, Jesus fulfills his promise not to leave his disciples orphans. In the Holy Spirit, Jesus' successor, who will abide with the Church forever, the people of God are never without religious leadership or guidance, never without God's saving presence among us.

To console his disciples, Jesus also promised to come back to them. This was an important promise, but the early Church misunderstood it, thinking in terms of the Second Coming when Jesus would appear triumphantly at the end of the world and right all wrongs. The early Church was facing brutal persecutions from both the Jewish and the Roman authorities and many of its members were sorely disappointed that Jesus delayed in coming to save them. Like many people today, the early Church was asking, "Where is God now, when we need him?"

In today's Gospel segment John writes to assure the early Christians that Jesus did keep his promise, that he did in fact return in the Resurrection, and that he did appear to many of the faithful to prove he had conquered death once and for all, as is amply well attested in Scripture. Moreover, for those who joined the Church after the Ascension and shared in none of the post-resurrection appearances, Jesus' words assure them that if they love him and keep his commandments, he will always remain with them. He assures all generations of Christians who keep his commandments, "You will realize that I am in my Father and you are in me and I am in you."

Today's Gospel passage shows God's great love for us, the members of his Church. Not only did he send his Son to live among us and show us the way, but after Jesus' Ascension he also sent the Holy Spirit to continue the work of Jesus on earth, to "enable" us to continue following in Jesus' footsteps and living as children of God. Thus all through the history of the Church, God has always been with us, first in the person of Jesus, then in the Holy Spirit. We have much to be grateful for, indeed, and much to do to show our gratitude.

Jesus Ascends into Heaven

Jesus left the world the way he came into it: quietly, without fuss, in the presence of only a few who were especially dear to him. As we note in today's event, the early Church in general, which consisted chiefly of Jewish converts, and Matthew in particular, who was writing largely for a Jewish audience, were quick to see similarities between Jesus, the greatest figure in the New Testament, and Moses, the greatest figure in the Old Testament. Just as God revealed himself to Moses on a mountain (Mount Sinai), so Jesus revealed himself to his disciples in the Transfiguration on a mountain (Mount Tabor). Just as Moses first taught the law from a mountain (Mount Sinai), so Jesus first taught the fulfillment of the law in the Sermon on the Mount. Now we are reminded of similarities in their departures from this world.

In Deuteronomy, the last of the five books of the Torah, attributed to Moses himself, at the very end of the book, chapter 34, we read that Moses ascended Mount Nebo just before he died. There God showed him the Holy Land stretched out before him, the Promised Land that Moses would not be allowed to enter because he had doubted God at Meribah. Moses then dies on the mountain and is buried in the hills, but Deuteronomy concludes by adding that to this day no one knows where Moses is buried. This fueled speculation among pious Jews that Moses had been taken up into heaven like Elijah, his body too important to return to the earth. In today's Gospel, Matthew is quick to point out that Jesus too was on a mountain when he was taken up into heaven, again similar to Moses and suggesting a reward for the very special life he led and the good he did.

Before departing, Jesus tells his disciples, "All power in heaven and on earth has been given to me." Up until the time of Jesus, such full power and authority had resided with Moses and the Mosaic Law he left behind. With the coming of Jesus, that power and authority passed to Jesus and was transformed and brought to completion. In Jesus the Law has been fulfilled and come to perfection. Moses' primitive ethic, an eye for an eye, a tooth for a tooth, introduced to curb the prevalent Mideast excesses of retribution and revenge, has been superseded by the far loftier and more demanding ethic: love your neighbor as yourself, and turn the other cheek. What Moses began, Jesus has brought to completion.

In his final command to baptize all nations, Jesus makes three things clear. (1) Baptism now replaces circumcision as the introduction and sign of incorporation into God's family. (2) Jesus' disciples are not to be passive recipients but active spreaders of the Gospel message. We are all missioned by our Baptism to spread the good news. (3) Salvation is no longer restricted to the Jewish people but open to all nations and all people of every race, color, and nationality. God's mission for the Church is now truly universal.

What are we to learn from the Ascension? The Creed tells us, "He ascended into heaven and is seated at the right hand of the Father." To the modern mind this connotes separation: his task done, Jesus is now at home with his Father, far removed from the turmoil of the modern world. Yet the Creed has the exact opposite intention. In ancient times, to sit at the right hand of someone meant the person had the other person's ear and therefore some influence with him. Sitting at the right hand of the king, for instance, was reserved for the queen, the highest ranking dignitary, or the specially invited guest — people who had access to and so could most easily sway the king. This notion of Jesus ascending to heaven and sitting at the right hand of the Father, then, was meant to convey that Jesus is now actively interceding for us with the Father, and that his role in the Church, far from having ceased, has rather intensified and switched in focus.

The message of the Ascension is, now that Jesus has returned to heaven, he is closer to us than ever. When Jesus was among us, he was limited by his physical body to a single place at a single time. With a human body circumscribed in time and space, he could not be everywhere. After his death and resurrection, however, he is no longer constrained by the limitations of a mortal body and continues to do good for the Church by interceding for us in heaven. In his stead, he sends the Holy Spirit, the third Person of the Blessed Trinity, to be with us. Thus, the triune God maintains an active presence and participation in today's world and Church through the Holy Spirit, while God the Son remains at the Father's right hand interceding for us. In short, far from speaking of God's withdrawal or retreat from the world, the Ascension actually signals more intensive involvement on two fronts, with Jesus interceding for us in heaven and the Holy Spirit actively engaged in the work of the Church on earth.

Matthew began his Gospel with reference to Emmanuel: God is with us. He ends his Gospel with Jesus' promise to be with us always. Thus, Matthew begins and ends his Gospel with the notion of God always with us in the person of Jesus Christ. A beautiful thought for Ascension Day.

The Great High Priestly Prayer

In the Old Testament it was common for great figures like Jacob and Moses to deliver a farewell address before they died. In it they typically did three things. (1) They praised God for his goodness to them. (2) They asked their followers to remain true to God and his Covenant. (3) They prayed for God's blessings on those they were leaving behind. In the New Testament, Jesus is no exception. He too gives a farewell address. John records it in chapters 14-16, at the Last Supper, the night before Jesus died.

Today, the Seventh Sunday of Easter, we read from the conclusion of that farewell address. It is fittingly called the Great High Priestly Prayer and it appears in John 17. It is particularly poignant because, for all practical purposes, it contains the last thoughts and words of Jesus just before he died. Scripture records that he spoke very little thereafter, preferring silence even at Pilate's questioning in the Roman Praetorium. In the Great High Priestly Prayer, Jesus prays first for himself, which we read today in Cycle A, then for his disciples, which we read in Cycle B, then for all Christians, which we read in Cycle C.

While John never records the Our Father in his Gospel, Jesus' final prayer adheres closely to it. Jesus calls God "Father," blesses God's name, asks that God's will be done, and prays for deliverance from the evil one. Today's passage is difficult and can be confusing to those unfamiliar with John's theology and terminology. I'd like simply to comment on six different parts that might otherwise cause confusion.

1. *The hour has come.* In John "hour" consistently refers to the time of Jesus' death and resurrection. Recall the first miracle at Cana. Mary informs Jesus they have no more wine, hoping he will help. Jesus replies enigmatically, "My hour has not yet come," meaning the time for his exaltation on the Cross where he will

finally be revealed as truly God's Son. In John's theology the death of Jesus is inexorably linked to the resurrection. The two form a single event and can never be separated: one the beginning, the other the end. That is why the crucifixion is always a moment of exaltation in John, never one of defeat, for it is the prelude to and culminates in the resurrection. One follows the other as assuredly as night follows day.

2. *May your Son give glory to you*. Glory in the Old Testament means a manifestation of God's love or saving power (Nb 14:22). Here Jesus prays that by freely laying down his life to save humankind, he will glorify the Father by revealing God's great love for the world. As John tells us, "God so loved the world that he did not spare his only Son." And as Jesus says, "Greater love than this no man has that he lay down his life for his friends." Moreover, by his perfect obedience to his Father's will, Jesus also glorifies God by showing he is truly the Son of God, the one who does God's will perfectly. Three times in the desert the devil began his temptation of Jesus with the words, "If you are the Son of God," and three times Jesus refused to follow Satan. Here Jesus fulfills God's will perfectly, even to the point of death, thus showing all of us how to act as God's children, putting God's will first and not our own.

3. *Give glory to your Son*. Jesus also prays that God will give glory to him. This is a prayer that God answers with the resurrection of Jesus. God in turn glorifies Jesus by raising him from the dead, showing unequivocally that death no longer has any power over him. And as God has raised Jesus from the dead, so he promises to raise all who believe in Jesus so that they might share eternal life with him. As Jesus has glorified God by his perfect compliance to his will, so God has glorified Jesus by raising him triumphantly from the dead, never to die again, the first fruits of those who believe.

4. *Eternal life is to know the only true God*. Some erroneously conclude from this that to know God and believe in him is enough.

Good works are not necessary. But to the Semitic mind, "know" means much more than cognitional awareness. To know someone means to have an intimate personal relationship with that person. As Genesis tells us, Adam "knew" his wife and she conceived a son. So it is not enough simply to know God and believe in him, we must form a loving relationship with him in our lifetime, by conforming our lives and dreams to his will, so that one day we will be happy with him forever.

5. *Those you gave me.* To the Calvinist, this speaks of pre-destination: God pre-selecting those who will be saved. In John, however, "those you gave me" means simply those who were receptive of God's grace, those who accepted God's gracious invitation and cooperated with it, those who were open to Jesus, docile to his message, and willing to put it into practice. In John's theology, God extends the grace of salvation to all, but all do not accept it, preferring to remain in darkness instead. Jesus refers to those who do accept it as God's gift to him.

6. *I pray not for the world.* The "world" in John does not refer to the human race collectively. John uses the "world" distinctly and consistently to denote those who prefer the things of earth to things of heaven, those who refuse to accept God's ways and prefer to follow their own will instead. The "world" in John connotes those who obstinately refuse to accept Jesus or his message and so deliberately exclude themselves from God's saving plan. This reveals another facet of John's theology. In John, Jesus condemns no one. It is the individual who condemns him- or herself by not accepting God's Son.

Descent of the Holy Spirit

Pentecost is called the birthday or the beginning of the Church. It marks the point in history after the Resurrection when the Holy Spirit descended on the Apostles and both empowered and emboldened them to take up the mission of Jesus, to go out to all the world and preach the Gospel.

Pentecost, which we celebrate to commemorate the Descent of the Holy Spirit upon the Apostles and the early Church, was itself a major Jewish feast and a Canaanite feast prior to that. The Canaanites were the original inhabitants of the Holy Land. At this time of year in Palestine the wheat harvest comes in. The Canaanites annually held an agricultural festival to celebrate the harvest. The festival was so popular and ingrained that when the Jews conquered the Holy Land they continued the festival but made it one of thanksgiving to Yahweh both for the wheat harvest and for the gift of the Covenant on Mount Sinai. Pentecost literally means 50th and the feast was celebrated on the 50th day or seven weeks after Passover.

The Jewish feast of Pentecost explains why so many people of different countries and languages were in Jerusalem at the time of the Descent of the Holy Spirit, as we read in Acts today. Mosaic Law (Ex 23:14) required all adults near Jerusalem to worship at the Temple three times a year: Passover, Pentecost, and Tabernacles. Jews living more than three days away were expected to come whenever they could; those far away, at least once in their lifetimes. Hence the crowds speaking different tongues.

The presence of so many people speaking diverse tongues sets the Christian feast of Pentecost in the context of the Tower of Babel. In Genesis, chapter 11, we read that as the human race increased and multiplied, they continued to speak the same language. But they grew proud over time with their accomplishments and wanted to make a tower that would reach straight into the heavens, a symbol for wanting to be like God himself, the same sin Adam and Eve had succumbed to earlier in the Garden of Eden when they ate of the symbolically forbidden fruit. So God came and confused their language so they could no longer understand each other, and scattered them over the face of the earth. Humankind tried to make itself the equal of God and ended up scattered and confused, unable to communicate with God or each other.

The coming of the Spirit on Pentecost reverses the world situation since Babel. With the coming of the Holy Spirit, the people and pilgrims in Jerusalem, though of different languages and "confused" at first, can all understand the Apostles' message. What sin and pride had split apart is reunited by the Spirit.

We are told that tongues of fire appeared over the heads of the Apostles. Fire in the ancient world was used to purify precious metals such as gold and silver and to strengthen baser metals such as iron. So fire became a symbol for purity and strength. Recall God spoke to Moses from a burning bush (Ex 3:2). The tongues of fire symbolize that henceforth the Apostles would speak the unadulterated word of God with vigor while being understood by all. St. Jude is generally portrayed with a tongue of fire over his head, possibly suggesting he was a particularly effective preacher of the word of God.

We read two accounts of Pentecost today, one from Luke's Acts, the other from John's Gospel. Both accounts use creation imagery to suggest that Pentecost involves a new creation. In Genesis we read there was wind and chaos before the Spirit hovered over the abyss and the work of creation began. So today we read in Acts there was a violent wind before the Spirit descended on the Apostles. In Genesis, when God created Adam and Eve, he communicated life by breathing into them, giving them human form and making them to his own image. This means God gave them a mind so they might know him, a will so they might freely choose to love him, and an immortal soul. With these gifts of mind, will, and immortal soul, which no other species has, God made humankind the pinnacle of all creation. In today's Gospel from John, Jesus breathes on the Apostles at Pentecost and gives them new life, the supernatural gift of grace which brings the indwelling of the Holy Spirit. This makes us children of God and no longer merely creatures of God. Hence Pentecost marks a new creation. It is the beginning of a new and higher order.

Jesus also gives the Apostles the power to forgive sin. Having given us grace and new life as children of God, yet knowing full well that many would stumble and fall due to human folly or frailty, Jesus gives the Church the power to forgive sin. This enables the Church to restore the fallen to God's love and help us continue to live as God's children despite human weakness and ineptitude.

So today as we celebrate this great feast of Pentecost, let us thank God for the gift of the Spirit and the continuing love of the Trinity for humankind, for the Father who created us, the Son who came to redeem us, and the Holy Spirit who continues to dwell within us and sanctify the members of the Church. Let us be aware of our call to bring to completion the work the Spirit began on Pentecost with the words of Jesus, "As the Father has sent me, so I send you." As members of Christ's Body, the Church, by our Baptism, we are all called to spread the good news of the Gospel. In the second reading (1 Cor), St. Paul reminds us we all have different gifts. But whatever those gifts be, let us use them freely and generously that our love and service of others will make God's love known to all the world and help them better know, love, and serve the Lord.

The Mystery of the Trinity

Today is the Feast of the Most Holy Trinity, the central dogma of Christianity. In the Trinity we profess there is but one God yet three divine Persons in that one God: Father, Son, and Holy Spirit. The Trinity is called a mystery because the human mind cannot fully grasp or understand it and this often presents a problem to the western mind. People from the east, like the Hindus, realize that any idea the human mind can form of God is bound to be inadequate. So when they pray before a statue representing God, they apologize to God for having to adore him in this particular form when he is in fact formless, for having to worship him in this particular temple when he is in fact everywhere, and for being too limited as humans to really comprehend him. Westerners, however, feel that reason should explain everything of importance. So if there is a God, we should be able to understand him.

Many a saint and theologian has tried to explain the Trinity. To Irish farmers St. Patrick used the image of a shamrock: one stem, three leaves, yet one plant. To people in the Renaissance, St. Ignatius compared the Trinity to three notes comprising a single chord or sound. Others have used the image of water which can assume three distinct forms: steam when heated, ice when frozen, and liquid at room temperature. Still others have used the image of the sun which also manifests itself to us below in three distinct forms: heat, light, and energy.

I prefer a scriptural approach to the Trinity. God never chose to give us a theological treatise on his nature. But he did reveal himself to us in history and that revelation is recorded in Scripture. If we look at Scripture from start to finish, we see that God first revealed himself to us as Father, then as Son, and finally as Holy Spirit.

Starting at the beginning of the Old Testament, we see God

acting as Father and Creator. He created the world and all that is in it, the sun and the moon and the stars. Without him nothing came to be. We see the Father's great love for humankind, creating us in his own image and giving us dominance over all the world. We see humankind disobey our heavenly Father and foolishly cut ourselves off from God. Despite human sinfulness, God the loving Father cannot and does not remain distant. He makes a covenant with Abraham and watches over his descendants. When they are enslaved in Egypt, God sends Moses to the Pharaoh with the command, "Let my son Israel go." He leads them through the desert for forty years of testing where he gives them the Ten Commandments and enters into a new covenant with them. Once settled comfortably in the Promised Land, however, the Israelites once again begin to stray from God, as humankind is wont to do. When they do, God sends the prophets with a consistent message: God is a God of love who wants his people back; reform your lives and return home to God your Father. All through these many centuries we see God as a loving Father reaching out to reconcile with his wayward, forgetful children, the self same he created out of nothing.

Finally in the fullness of time, God sends his Son. God the Father, as it were, withdraws into the background and God the Son takes center stage in the drama of salvation history. The Old Testament closes and the New Testament begins with the four Gospels. There we see Jesus spending his life teaching and preaching, declaring God's unconditional love for us and calling all to repentance and forgiveness of sin. He shows us by word, deed, and example how to live as God's children, ultimately laying down his life for us.

With the death and resurrection of Jesus, revelation ceases and is over. As the Word of God, Jesus is the perfect revelation of the Father. There could be no better. But still the disciples were unable to comprehend who Jesus really was or grasp the full significance of his message. Many found it difficult to accept the resurrection without firsthand experience; many, too, had no inkling of the divinity of Jesus. So God sent the Holy Spirit to bring to fulfillment the work begun by Jesus. The Holy Spirit enlightens the early Church and helps them to come to understand and accept all that Jesus had revealed. Just as Jesus played the central role in the beginning of the New Testament or the four Gospels, so we see the Holy Spirit dominating the end of the New Testament or the Acts of the Apostles, which chronicles the history, development, and expansion of the Church after the ascension of Jesus. The Holy Spirit thus signifies the continuing and abiding presence of God in the world today, helping the Church to understand and put into practice the teaching of Jesus.

So today as we celebrate the Feast of the Most Holy Trinity, let us give thanks to God the Father who created us, to God the Son who redeemed us, and to God the Holy Spirit who continues to live within us and the Church as a life-giving, sanctifying force. And as a practical point to bring the Trinity into our lives, each night before we fall asleep, let us think briefly of the good we received during the day and thank God the Father for creating it for us. Let us think briefly of any wrong we did during the day and ask God the Son to forgive us for it through the merits of his passion and death. And let us think briefly of what we have to do tomorrow and ask the Holy Spirit to lead us and guide us so that what we do as true Christians will reflect our love for God and each other.

The Experience of Fr. Walter Ciszek, S.J.

Today is the Feast of Corpus Christi which translates literally from the Latin as "the Body of Christ." In the Eucharist we receive Jesus, body and blood, soul and divinity. Since today's feast honors the Eucharist in a special way, Corpus Christi is usually transcribed into English as the Body and Blood of Christ. Each year as we celebrate this glorious feast I am reminded of Fr. Walter Ciszek, S.J., a saintly man who died at Fordham on December 8, 1984 and whose cause has already been introduced to Rome for canonization. Fr. Ciszek was an American citizen whom the Soviets long imprisoned yet always denied they held until they needed a bargaining chip some twenty-five years later to offer in exchange for the convicted atom spy Klaus Fuchs. Fr. Ciszek subsequently wrote two books, *With God in Russia*, a factual account, and *He Leadeth Me*, a spiritual journal.

Fr. Ciszek was born in Pennsylvania and joined the Jesuits as a young man. In response to a papal appeal he volunteered to serve in the Eastern Rite while still a seminarian and was ordained just before the outbreak of World War II. He was sent to eastern Poland but soon found himself cut off from much of his flock when the Nazis and Soviets partitioned Poland. He elected to go behind Soviet lines to help those cut off. With vast numbers of refugees flowing in all directions, he assumed he would never be noticed. But he could not have been more wrong. The Soviets knew who he was and arrested him on the spot as an alleged Vatican spy. He was sent to the dreaded Lubianka prison in Moscow and held in solitary confinement for five years. During all that time he never saw a human face or heard a human voice save for his interrogators who worked on him night and day. After five years they finally broke him down. He signed a false confession. It was the lowest point in his life. He felt he had betrayed God, Church, and country. He even thought of suicide. But from the ashes came hope. He realized he had depended too much on his own strength and resources and not enough on God. He put himself completely at God's disposal and when he did, he was filled with a profound peace that the Soviets could never wrest from him again.

From Lubianka he was sent to Siberia where he would spend the next fifteen years at hard labor in the Gulag prison system. There he had to work long hours each day in sub-zero weather on starvation rations. The work was exhausting, unending. One project required prisoners to cut hundreds of miles through solid rock using only pickaxes and shovels to create a canal for ocean-going vessels. Another had them felling and clearing vast tracts of dense forests with no more than handsaws and axes. The worst was the salt mines where most prisoners died within months, their lungs eaten up by the dank air.

To me the most memorable parts of his books revolved around the Eucharist, from the complete and debilitating absence of the Eucharist during his Lubianka confinement, leading in part to his collapse, to his heroic and often futile attempts to celebrate the Eucharist inside the Gulag camps. Nuns who had been driven out of convent life freely moved to Siberia to help the unfortunate prisoners in whatever way they could. One way was to smuggle into the camps the hosts and wine necessary for Mass. Fr. Ciszek's happiest moments were receiving such parcels. But they were also fraught with danger. Anyone involved in a Mass would be severely punished, his sentence stiffened. The safest way for Fr. Ciszek to offer Mass was under the covers with everyone else asleep. But he rarely did so because no one else could attend.

In those days one had to be fasting from midnight to receive Communion, so Fr. Ciszek had to organize the night before. Prisoners received only two meals a day. A thin gruel and a crust of bread in the morning, a pasty soup and more bread at night. Anyone signing up for Mass thus signed away one of two meager meals for the day and would have to do a full day's work on an empty stomach with no food for 24 hours. Yet there was never a shortage of volunteers, so eager were they to receive the Eucharist. The best time for Mass was at noon when worked stopped so the guards could eat. The prisoners got nothing. They simply grabbed what rest they could. It was at this time that Fr. Ciszek would try to slip out of sight with his group to say Mass by moving farther into the forest or deeper into the mine. But if the guards proved vigilant or other prisoners grew inquisitive, it was futile. They had skipped breakfast in vain.

It was at these unfortunate times that prisoners revealed even greater heroic mettle and devotion. The group had the option of abandoning the plan or trying again at night when the other prisoners were distracted by dinner. Most voted to try again even though it meant also skipping dinner and thus going without food for 36 hours. Their desire for the Eucharist was so strong that physical nourishment paled in comparison, notwithstanding the fact they were badly undernourished and cruelly overworked.

Today as we celebrate the Feast of Corpus Christi, let us thank God for the gift of the Eucharist which we celebrate at Mass each day and for his abiding presence with us in the Blessed Sacrament in every church in the world. Let us pray for a deeper appreciation of the Eucharist in our lives so that like Soviet prisoners in the Gulag we will receive Our Lord with greater devotion and more intense longing. Let us also pray in thanksgiving that we have never experienced persecution or suffering for our faith in our country and ask God always to keep us free, responsible, and grateful.

The Call of Matthew

At this point in Matthew's Gospel Jesus has left the small, sleepy town of Nazareth in southern Galilee where he was raised and centered his base of operations at Capernaum, a bustling city situated to the northeast on the shore of the Sea of Galilee. Both Matthew and Mark report that Jesus often crossed the sea from one side to the other. On the western shore lay Galilee with its largely Jewish population; on the eastern shore was the region of the ten cities called the Decapolis with a predominantly pagan population. The frequent crisscrossing of the sea with miracles performed on both shores suggests that at this point in his ministry in particular Jesus was dividing his time and energy among Jews and pagans alike. As a prelude to today's passage, for instance, Jesus cured two demoniacs in the pagan region of the Gadarenes on the east bank, followed immediately by the cure of a paralytic on the west bank in Jewish territory that explicitly involved a forgiveness of the sick man's sins.

Coming smack upon the heels of two such dramatic healings involving both body and soul, Jew and foreigner, today's Gospel account continues and expands upon the theme of mercy and universal outreach. Jesus invites Matthew, a tax collector, to follow him. In choosing a tax collector for one of his special disciples, one despised for his choice of occupation and branded a sinner for his line of work, Jesus dramatically demonstrated the gratuitous nature of any such call, the utter graciousness of God's gift, and the overwhelming unworthiness of anyone so called. Yet such a call is simply a vocation and, as Christians, we too have been called through our Baptism to follow Jesus more closely.

Tax collectors are never popular. People generally find it hard to warm to those who commandeer large chunks of their income. At the time of Jesus the Jews had added cause to hate tax representatives for both political and religious reasons. Politically, the Jewish people had been conquered and subjugated by the Romans. Their tax revenues now went primarily to support the Roman occupation of their land and to facilitate and further Rome's continued imperialistic ambitions. Religiously, the Romans were a pagan people with a pantheon of imaginary deities that included the reigning emperor and his predecessor. Tax revenues were used in part to construct temples to the various Roman gods and emperors. This to the Jewish mind was the crudest form of idolatry and proved to be a constant irritant to Jewish sensibilities.

The role of the tax collector was further complicated by Rome's method of collecting taxes. Rome wanted the revenue, to be sure, but it did not want to waste its time or dirty its hands in collecting it. So Rome simply decided how much it wanted from a district and leased the contract out to the highest bidder. The person winning the contract then had the task of collecting enough taxes to pay off the bid plus a cushion to insure a reasonable profit for himself. With the tax collector working to pay off his investment and secure a profit for himself, Rome had good reason to be sure of his diligence while the Jews had even stronger reason to fear his zeal and greed. Since the work involved close cooperation with the Roman authorities and helped them strengthen their control of the occupied land, the Jewish people also came to regard tax collectors as collaborators with Rome in its suppression of Israel. They hated them both for enriching themselves at the cost of their fellow countrymen and for aiding and abetting the pagan power of Rome.

Taxes in the Roman Empire were varied and ubiquitous. Some commentators surmise the type of taxes Matthew collected from the location. Today's Gospel is set in the environs of Capernaum which was close to the border between Galilee and Trachonitis. On the death of Herod the Great, who ruled during the Infancy Narrative, his kingdom was divided up into four parts. One of his sons, Herod Antipas, was given the province of Galilee; another son,

Herod Philip, also known as Herod the tetrarch, received the region of Trachonitis. Both were vassals of Rome as their father was before them. Anyone crossing the border between Herod Antipas' jurisdiction in Galilee and Philip's rule in Trachonitis would be liable for custom duties and road fees. Some suggest, therefore, that Matthew was likely in the direct employ of Herod Antipas gathering levies from travelers and merchants for border crossings and road use. With Capernaum directly on the trade routes between Egypt and the East, it was likely a lucrative business.

In today's Gospel after inviting Matthew to follow him despite his profession, Jesus then goes to Matthew's house to share a meal with him and his friends who were also commonly regarded as sinners. The Pharisees strove for perfect observance of the Mosaic Law. They regarded anyone who did not observe the smallest letter of the law as a sinner, even shepherds and camel drivers whose work often kept them far from the Temple for public worship and short of water for frequently required ritual purifications. In their minds anyone even coming into contact with a Gentile was rendered ritually impure. So you can imagine their consternation when Jesus, a self-professed teacher of Israel, sat down at table with just such a group. In answer to their challenge, Jesus refers to today's first reading from Hosea (6:6) where God calls for *hesed* and not sacrifice, where *hesed* means both mercy and steadfast love. Jesus makes clear he came to save all people. Discipleship no longer depends on genealogy but on each one's faith response.

Missioning the Apostles

In today's Gospel the word "Apostle" is used for the first time. "Apostle" in Greek means "one who is sent out." And here we see the Apostles being sent out to preach the good news that the kingdom of God is at hand in the person and mission of Jesus Christ. Matthew is careful to mention that there are twelve Apostles, a number historically important in the history of Israel and the Church. Just as the twelve tribes of Israel, God's chosen people, descended from the twelve sons of Jacob, so will God's new people, the Church, spring from the twelve Apostles whom Jesus had chosen to be his emissaries.

The Gospel tells us Jesus sent his Apostles to the "lost sheep of the house of Israel." In biblical times this meant, not evildoers angry with God, but ordinary people who drifted away from the practice of their religion and felt alienated from God. Remember in the time of Jesus, Judaism was dominated by the Pharisees and the Pharisees insisted on the strictest interpretation of the Mosaic Law. They added so many prescriptions and codicils to the law that the ordinary person could not possibly know, let alone remember, them all. Yet the Pharisees held failure to observe even the least letter of the law meant failure to observe the whole law. No wonder ordinary people who had families to raise and livings to make, felt alienated and drifted away. It was these ordinary people who were like sheep without shepherds or leaders, a virtual harvest of souls waiting to be gathered in.

In sending the Apostles out, Jesus empowers them and commissions them to "cure the sick, raise the dead, heal the leprous, expel demons," words carefully patterned after Isaiah's prophecy concerning the Messiah, which Jesus publicly claimed to fulfill: "The blind see, the deaf hear, the lame walk, and the poor have the good news preached to them." Too often we misunderstand these words. When Isaiah spoke, he was speaking figuratively. When the Messiah comes, Isaiah tells us, those who are blind to God's plan for them will finally have their eyes opened, those who are deaf to God's call will finally hear, those who are halt in following God's ways will take great strides, those who are mired in sin will repent. When Jesus came, he fulfilled Isaiah's prophecy both figuratively and literally. Besides awakening their spirits, he also cured their physical ailments. But the figurative or spiritual meanings were always primary. Jesus came to save us once and for all from sin, not physical sickness. The physical cures took place in large part to assure his audience that if he could restore people physically from such terrible afflictions as leprosy and death, which all could see, he also had the power to free them from sin, which they could not see.

In today's Gospel Jesus gives the Apostles similar power, for similar reasons. But unfortunately it diminishes the intensity of the Gospel message for us today who are the descendants of the Apostles and members of the Church. Through our Baptism we are also commissioned to go out to preach the good news, to heal, to cure, to raise up, to help all people. But without the special power bestowed on the Apostles, we feel inadequate to the task, overwhelmed by the assignment. And the reason is that we take the Gospel passage literally when its meaning for us is primarily poetic. Jesus is not asking us to restore physical sight to the blind, or hearing to the deaf, or life to the deceased. He is asking us to help open the eyes of the people around us to the beauty of God's love and plan for them, to help people open their ears to the voice of God who never ceases calling them, to help people who have given up on religion and things spiritual to awaken once again to the love of God around them.

For this you don't need a soapbox or a pulpit. The kitchen table at home, the water cooler at the office, the 19th hole, wherever people gather, you can exercise compassion, show a willingness to listen, be unafraid to share your views and values and most of all the gift of faith we have all received. Giving sight to the blind need be nothing more than giving someone with low self esteem a reason to feel good about him- or herself. A well placed word or a simple affirmation of what Christians hold to be right or wrong may well help someone otherwise deaf to the Spirit to hear the Church's teaching on an important issue for the first time. Being willing to forgive often dissolves the leprosy of rage and grudge-cherishing.

I close with a family story that bears upon today's Gospel. I had a grand aunt who married a Jewish man. It was a very happy marriage that produced two children and many grandchildren, all raised as Catholics. My grand aunt prayed night and day for her husband's conversion and had the whole family making novenas and lighting candles for that intention, but nothing ever happened. Then in the twilight of their years when they were living in a large house with their extended family, a nun came to the door one day to take the parish census when they were all out but Uncle Abe. He invited her in and tried to help her. She asked first the names and ages of all in the household. Then she asked if they were all Catholic. "All but me," answered Uncle Abe. "And you, why aren't you a Catholic?" she inquired. "Because no one ever asked me," he replied. She signed him up right then and there for instructions and he was baptized soon after. You could have knocked my aunt over with a feather. She and the whole family were delighted, but no one had ever thought to ask!

Whoever Acknowledges Me Before Men

Today's Gospel is the continuation of last week's Gospel in which Jesus chose his twelve Apostles and sent them out to proclaim that the kingdom of God was at hand. To understand the meaning and structure of today's passage, we need to review and extend some of the ideas developed last week. Recall that Matthew was Jewish, writing primarily for his own people, and trying to convince them that Jesus, as the Messiah, surpassed all the figures in the Old Testament, even Moses, the greatest teacher, leader, and law-giver. To Moses were attributed the first five books of the Old Testament, collectively called the Torah and universally hailed as the most sacred in all the Old Testament. To highlight the similarities between Jesus and Moses, Matthew also divides his Gospel account of Jesus into five sections or books. Each of Matthew's five books is in turn divided into two parts: a narrative setting forth the deeds that Jesus did, followed by an extended discourse detailing the teachings of Jesus to explain what he did. What we read today comes from the second book of Matthew. To see the parallelism with Moses, we need only note that the second book of the Torah, called the Book of Exodus, begins with the words, "These are the names of the twelve tribes of Israel." Matthew's second book by way of comparison begins with the words, "These are the names of the twelve Apostles."

The title of the Book of Exodus, with which today's passage is being compared, literally means "a departure." Exodus tells the story of the Jewish people's departure from Egypt and their travails as they trudged through the desert in search of the promised land. Just as God sent the twelve tribes of Israel out of Egypt, so Matthew's second book tells us Jesus sends out his twelve Apostles on mission. And just as the Jewish people encountered trials and tribulations on their journey, so Jesus tells his disciples they can expect to find similar upheavals in pursuing their assignment.

Today's particular passage is from the discourse section of Matthew's second book. In this discourse, Jesus spells out what his disciples can expect. The Jewish people faced considerable obstacles during the exodus. Jesus likewise cautions his disciples they will meet stiff opposition in their task. They will be hailed before kings, governors, and the Sanhedrin to defend their mission. The Jewish people were often rejected and persecuted in their pursuit of the promised land. Similar treatment awaits his disciples, Jesus warns, in spreading the news of the kingdom. In such cases they must be prepared to shake the dust of the towns from their feet. The unfamiliar is intrinsically frightening. The trepidation the early Church faced in fanning out among unfamiliar peoples to disseminate the Gospel was not unlike the uneasiness Israel experienced in its trek across the desert. Fear of the unknown always remains a basic human instinct.

So Jesus tells his disciples not to be afraid. He says it at the beginning, middle, and end of the passage. As God helped the Israelites through the desert to the promised land, so Jesus implies God will help the Church in being true to its mission. He reminds them and us that God cares even for the simple sparrow and we, as disciples of Jesus, are worth more than many sparrows in God's sight. Difficulties will come, but God will always be there. In effect, Jesus is telling us not to be paralyzed by fear. If Jesus suffered persecution in his lifetime, his followers can expect no better. But as God supported Jesus in every adversity and ultimately raised him triumphant from the dead, so God will be with us in our trials. And if we prove victorious, he will also raise us up to eternal life. Jesus tells us bluntly there is no need to fear those who can kill only the body. Christians must maintain a positive attitude to prove they are good disciples.

Years ago psychologists at the University of California studied why some people succeed while other people with equal talents and opportunities fail. Working with 1700 students over six years, they paired people with the same IQ's, GPA's, incomes, etc. They concluded the single most important factor in identifying future success or failure was a strong self-image free of fear or doubt. Those with a strong self-image were more likely to succeed; those with a poor self-image, more prone to failure. Others then carried the study over into religion. Christianity tells us to love God and love neighbor. Who is most likely to do this? The answer they found was the same: the person with a strong positive self-image free of crippling doubts and fears. Why? Christianity demands love and love is a gift of self. Those who don't think much of themselves are reluctant to make a gift of self. They hold back out of fear of rejection or ridicule.

Psychology Today later published a similar study of children under the age of six to predict their future success in life. The children were asked to draw pictures of themselves and explain the pictures. One picture was of a little girl. She drew herself as a prima ballerina, so large that she couldn't fit her tiara on the page. There was also very little room before the stage for the audience, whom she explained were cheering wildly. I concluded she had an ego bigger than herself. Another picture was by a little boy. He drew a tiny figure sitting quietly on a stool in the corner. Most of the canvas was bare. I deduced he was modest. When the final analyses came, was my face red! The professionals were happy with the girl. Her picture revealed a strong self-image surrounded by love — all she needed to face a hostile world. They feared for the boy. His sketch suggested low self-esteem; the near empty canvas, a void in his life. If children are going to love God, they have first to experience love in their lives. The more love, the better.

Take Up Your Cross

Today's Gospel is the conclusion of the tenth chapter of Matthew which we began to read two weeks ago. I would like to round out what we said then by adding something about Matthew's Gospel in general, then say something specific about the passage we read today.

The statements and teachings of Moses are found in the first five books of the Old Testament, known as the Pentateuch, the Torah, or simply the Law. The first five books were considered the most sacred in all the Old Testament. As I mentioned two weeks ago, in his Gospel Matthew arranges the statements and teachings of Jesus into five lengthy discourses or books. He does so deliberately to parallel the first five books of the Old Testament in order to show that the Gospel supersedes the Old Testament and that Jesus supersedes Moses, the greatest teacher, leader and law-giver in the Old Testament.

Matthew, chapter 10, marks the second discourse of Jesus. It parallels Exodus, the second book of the Old Testament. Two weeks ago when we read from the beginning of this chapter, we saw the first parallel. Exodus begins with the words, "These are the names of the twelve tribes of Israel," the twelve from which God's chosen people, Israel, descended. Matthew, chapter 10, begins with, "These are the names of the twelve Apostles," the twelve from whom Jesus' Church, the new Israel, will descend. Having read through the whole chapter now, we can see further parallels.

Exodus is primarily concerned with the departure of the Israelites from Egypt and their forty years of wandering in the desert where they were prepared and tested to see if they were truly worthy to become God's people. In sum, the Book of Exodus has two major themes: departure and preparation. The second discourse of Jesus in Matthew deals with sending out the Apostles to preach the

Gospel. But before they go, Jesus prepares them by telling them what they are to expect and what they are to say. Thus Matthew's second book or discourse also deals with the dual theme of departure and preparation.

There are also more specific parallels. In Exodus there are two outstanding moments. The first is God's giving the Ten Commandments to Moses on Mount Sinai in which God spells out what he expects of his people. The second is the promise of land which God will make available to the Jewish people and they will be able to call their own. God tells them if they keep the commandments, they will inherit the land. We have a series of commands and expectations, followed by a series of promises and rewards.

In the passage we just heard, Jesus also gives his disciples a series of commands. You must love me more than father and mother, you must be willing to take up your cross each day and follow me. Having given a series of commands, Jesus also promises a series of rewards. And the reward he promises is far greater than an earthly land or inheritance; it is the promise of eternal life in the kingdom of God. He also promises that anyone who helps another in spreading the Gospel will share in that person's reward. Helping a prophet means sharing a prophet's reward. Here we also see a series of commands and expectations, followed by the promise of rewards. This is a further indication of just how closely Matthew modeled this chapter of his Gospel on the Book of Exodus. He did so in order to suggest the superiority of Jesus and his message over Moses and all the Old Testament promises.

As for today's specific passage, it offers a good opportunity to understand how certain passages got into Scripture. Remember all the evangelists tell us that Jesus did and said far more than could be written down in the Gospel accounts. Why were certain things remembered and other things forgotten in the more than fifty years of oral tradition between the death of Jesus and the writing of the Gospels? Scripture scholars tell us that key events like the passion, death, and resurrection of Jesus were so central they were remem-

bered by all. But other events were recalled simply because they had special meaning for the early Church, making them relevant and often repeated. Today's passage offers two cases in point. Of all the sayings of Jesus why were those concerned with loving him more than family and taking up one's cross remembered? The answer is: both had a deep impact on the early Church.

When Matthew's Gospel was being written, the Church was being persecuted in Jerusalem. Those of Jewish origin who followed Jesus were being excommunicated from the synagogues and cut off from their religious, economic, political, and social base. Many came under pressure from their families to abandon Jesus and return to traditional Judaism lest they bring social and financial ruin on themselves and their loved ones. Consequently Jesus' warning not to love family members more than him had particular meaning given the concrete situation of the early Church and hence was likely remembered.

As for taking up one's cross, we need only recall that the Church in Rome was also undergoing persecution. Christians who refused to worship the emperor were thrown to the lions. One can imagine how people may have been tempted to equivocate or back away from a public stand, leading Christians to warn and support each other with Jesus' reference to the cross. It had deep meaning because it was the sign by which Jesus proved his love for us and for his Father and in the concrete situation of active religious persecution it was the sign of what could be expected of those who wanted to be true to Jesus.

My Yoke Is Easy

In today's Gospel Jesus says, "Learn from me for I am gentle and humble of heart." These were obviously virtues Jesus thought important for his followers. Unfortunately in our society today, however, gentleness and humility are no longer esteemed. They are rather despised, confused with being a door mat, lacking backbone, or being unable or unwilling to stand up and fight for one's self and one's rights. Self-assertiveness is much more highly prized, while violence is promoted and even glorified in movies, sporting events, and on TV. Partly as a result of ignoring this command of Jesus, violence has taken root in the land. We find it in our cities, our streets, even in our schools. Too often we read about the battered woman, the abused child, the discarded fetus. We ignore Jesus' teaching only at our peril.

In today's Gospel Jesus also says that what God has hidden from the learned and the clever, he has revealed to mere children. By "the learned and the clever," Jesus was clearly referring to those scribes and Pharisees who were smug in their knowledge of Scripture and the law, and felt there was nothing they could learn from the carpenter's son from Nazareth. They who thought they knew all about God and his revelation failed to recognize Jesus as the Word of God and the perfect manifestation of the Father. By "mere children," Jesus was not referring literally to tots and toddlers but to all who were childlike and willing to learn from those who could help them and advance their knowledge of God. This category figuratively included the poor and the humble, embracing in some instances even tax collectors and public sinners.

Another theme Jesus develops is that of a yoke. He says to us, "Take my yoke upon your shoulders." "Yoke" in the Old Testament was a symbol for the law, in the sense of the Mosaic Law and the precepts of God made known through revelation. These precepts are largely contained in the first five books of the Old Testament, called the Pentateuch, Torah, or simply the Law. Jewish law in Old Testament times was burdensome. The Torah alone contains 613 precepts. To these the scribes and Pharisees added hundreds of other man-made laws, later codified in the Talmud, which they maintained also had to be kept perfectly and in their entirety. To fail in even one of the least of these man-made precepts meant failure to keep the law in its entirety which they proclaimed was essential for salvation. The ordinary person could not possibly remember all of these commandments, however, let alone observe them. As a result, many felt overwhelmed by an impossible burden and situation and simply gave up. This is what Jesus meant when he complained that the scribes and Pharisees had placed heavy burdens on others' shoulders that were impossible to carry.

By way of contrast, Jesus says his yoke is easy, his burden light. Instead of the myriad commands the Pharisees prescribed, Jesus had earlier taken all the precepts of Old Testament law and summed them up into two: love of God and love of neighbor, making it easy for everyone to remember what God expected of them. And while love of God and love of neighbor can often be taxing and demanding, the command to do so is easy in the sense that it conforms both to our nature and to our purpose in life so that it is in fact the only way that will lead us to true happiness in this world and in the next. Those who accept the yoke of Jesus in the sense of the law of Jesus or the teaching of Jesus, will indeed be happy for they will be fulfilling their nature and their destiny.

A yoke literally is a harness put over the shoulders of oxen or beasts of burden to enable them to pull a plow or cart. The yoke in Old Testament times was made of wood and wood is an unyielding and non-forgiving substance. It has no give or take. So the yoke had to be fitted carefully to the animal and each animal had to have its individual yoke. An improper fit would quickly lead to chafing, irritation, abrasions, or lesions, any of which in the Mideast heat would soon cause ulcers and infections, disabling, crippling, or killing the animal. The image of the yoke that Jesus uses, therefore, is a beautiful reminder that the yoke Jesus assigns to each of us in life is specially fitted and individually tailored for us by God to fit our circumstances. Moreover, as a loving Father, God always apportions his grace to fit the condition.

In conclusion, by way of contrast to the Pharisees who had a "Do as I say, not as I do" attitude, Jesus was a "Do as I do" sort of person. He tells us simply, "Learn from me." We should be grateful we have a God who doesn't ask the impossible, a God who doesn't ask what he himself has not done before us in his life with us on earth. He has gone before us. He has shown us the way. He is the way, the truth, and the life, and we have only to model our life and our love on his, confident of his ever-present help and grace, to be happy one day with him forever in heaven. When joined to him, our yoke is easy, our burden light.

Parable of the Sower

Have you ever tried to tell the truth to someone who refused to listen? Worse, have you ever resisted the truth that someone tried to tell you? Have you ever tried to teach someone who didn't want to learn or was afraid to learn? Like an adult facing the computer for the first time? It's hard to overcome this resistance. Jesus faced the same problem. That's one reason why he resorted to parables.

In today's Gospel Jesus refers to Isaiah to answer the Apostles' query as to why he uses parables: "They look but do not see, hear but do not listen." Jesus was referring to people who deliberately turned a blind eye to him and the good works he was doing, a deaf ear to what he was saying. The scribes and Pharisees, for instance, had studied Scripture and the Mosaic Law in the best rabbinical schools. They felt they knew all there was to know about God and had nothing to learn from a carpenter's son from Nazareth. Many of the ordinary people were also comfortable with the old ways and traditions and did not want to see or get involved in change. So Jesus spoke to them in parables.

A parable is a story in which an element in the story is compared to the people in the audience, without the audience at first realizing the story is about them. As a teacher, Jesus knew how effective a good story was in capturing the audience's attention. Everyone loves a good story. A story is helpful in remembering the lesson, because everyone remembers a good story and likes to pass it on to others. A story, if apt, is also helpful in driving the point of the lesson home. More importantly to today's Gospel, a parable disarms the audience so they don't automatically put up defenses. In telling a story about people or things in general, the audience does not feel threatened. They can relax, enjoy the story, make critical judgments on the story's plot. It's only later when they reflect on the story that they realize it's about them.

To understand today's parable, we should know something of land allocation and farming in Palestine. In ancient Palestine, land was divided proportionately among the children. It was unlike the Irish and English system in which the entire estate was left to the oldest son. This was terribly inequitable, for the younger sons were then forced to migrate to make a living and the daughters had to be married off. But it was done to preserve the family's wealth and position intact. In Palestine the system was more equitable, but its drawback was that the land was fractured over time, with each subsequent generation getting smaller and smaller plots. Moreover the plots were frequently scattered and dispersed. When an estate was divided, each of the children would get a share of the best land, the mediocre land, and the poorest land. This meant that over time families were farming smaller and smaller plots widely dispersed from each other. This explains the great diversity in soil conditions in today's Gospel. To get the most from the land, farmers in ancient Palestine also learned to scatter the seed first and then plow it under later. They scattered seed everywhere in the hopes that whatever could possibly grow would grow. As many a modern day gardener knows, grass will often refuse to grow on carefully prepared sites and yet cheerfully spring up in cracks of the cement.

To understand the meaning of the parable, we have only to look at the Old Testament. There the prophets described God's saving activity in terms of sowing (Jr 31:27, Ho 2:25). So the sower is clearly God or Jesus himself. The two are the same. The seed is the word of God, God's teaching and revelation, whatever communication God has had with humankind. And the soil is the audience itself. The different degrees of receptivity among humankind are compared to different types of soil.

The parable can be interpreted in two ways. If it is truly the Parable of the Sower, the focus is on God and the main message is the universality and all-embracing outpouring of God's love; the liberality with which God sows the seeds of faith: indiscriminately, with great abundance, on the receptive and non-receptive alike. The point is God wants all to be saved and reaches out to all. The parable, however, might be better called the Parable of the Soil, for the major emphasis is on the different conditions of soil. Here Jesus is saying that the harvest depends not only on the sowing, which is generous to a fault, but on the quality of the soil on which the seed falls, which is the receptivity of the individual. The reason for varying responses to Jesus and God's message is due solely to human freedom, choice, and conditioning.

Jesus also offers comparisons. Some seed fell on soil that was packed down and impenetrable. This soil is like those who have hardened their hearts against God and turn a blind eye to his goodness. They simply will not let the word of God enter their hearts. The Pharisees might well have recognized themselves in this comparison. Then there is the seed that fell in shallow, rocky soil. It shot up but, with shallow roots, soon died. This refers to people who receive God's word enthusiastically but then hear of something else and move on or don't want to be bothered working at putting their faith into practice. There is also the seed that fell among thorns. This points to people who want to be good Christians but encounter other competing forces in their lives: money, power, prestige, comfort; and they eventually opt for the easy way out. Lastly there is the deep, rich soil in which the seed can grow and produce a harvest a hundredfold. Let us pray that we be like good, rich soil in all aspects and times of our lives.

Parables of Darnel, Mustard Seed, and Yeast

Today's Gospel consists of three parables. The first one puts the owner of the field in a "Catch 22" situation. An enemy has sown weeds known as darnel in his field. Darnel looks very much like wheat in its early stages of growth. To try to uproot it early is to risk uprooting the wheat instead. Later when it is distinguishable, its roots are intertwined with the wheat and it cannot be uprooted without destroying the wheat. The owner seems damned if he does and damned if he doesn't. But the owner proves far wiser. By allowing both to grow, he knows he will be able to distinguish between the wheat and the darnel at harvest time when he can easily reap the wheat for his barns and separate the darnel for kindling.

In last week's Gospel Jesus compared his audience to soil. In today's Gospel Jesus tells his audience that wheat and weeds will grow on the same soil. On the simplest level of the parable, Jesus is telling us that there is both good and bad within each of us and good and bad within his Church. His message is one of patience. Have patience with yourself and patience with the Church. Many wish to love God with all their heart and soul but find themselves frequently straying and falling. They wonder if they should stay within the Church. Jesus' answer is yes. If we cooperate with him, he will help the good in us to prevail, like the wheat over the weeds. Others are discouraged by the weakness or slowness of the Church. The parable tells them not to worry about or expect perfection everywhere but simply to be good themselves. God will eventually triumph and distinguish the good from the evil in the Church.

The early Church, many of whose members were city folk with little knowledge of farming, clearly preferred the allegory that follows the parable. An allegory gives a point by point meaning to all the elements in the story. In the allegory Jesus compares himself to the sower of the good seed. The devil is the sower of the bad seed.

Good and evil exist side by side in this world and it is frequently difficult to distinguish who is good and who is bad. The story tells us not to worry, and not to judge others. We could be mistaken. The point is that God will one day judge all of us. He can distinguish between good and evil, and no one escapes his judgment.

The next two parables concern a mustard seed and yeast. The mustard seed was a Jewish symbol for the smallest of elements. Small transgressions of the Law, for instance, were described in terms of a mustard seed. Today we would simply call them venial sins. The parable of the yeast was directed at women who had to bake bread fresh each day. They knew a small amount of yeast placed in dough would cause the dough to rise and expand. The point of these two parables is that from small things, large things grow. From a tiny seed, a large shrub grows, capable of sheltering the birds of the sky in its branches. With a little yeast, a small amount of dough can feed a whole family. In both parables the mustard seed and yeast are compared to faith. From small beginnings, the faith can grow within us and the Church.

The other common theme to both parables is that the growth that takes place is hidden. We cannot see or perceive how it takes place. The seed is buried in the ground and somehow above ground a shrub takes shape before our eyes. Yeast is kneaded into dough, and miraculously the dough begins to rise and expand. So, too, with faith. The Spirit is within us and the Church, even though we cannot see him, and he gives life and growth in ways that we frequently cannot perceive.

These parables were of great importance and consolation to the original disciples and early Church. They were called upon to spread the good news of Jesus Christ and salvation to all the world. Yet they felt small and insignificant, totally unsuited for the mission placed upon them. The parables taught them that through faith in Jesus and cooperation with the Spirit, God could and would accomplish great things through them.

All three parables have meaning for us today. We, too, often feel helpless and overwhelmed by our baptismal obligation to help spread the faith. The parables of the mustard seed and the yeast should help us recall that we are not called upon to act alone. The Spirit is within us and within the Church, like the mustard seed buried in the ground and the yeast kneaded into the dough, and it is through the Spirit that we and the Church will grow in the faith. Though we cannot see or perceive his presence, Jesus assures us he is truly with us through all time. With God's help our influence can have an impact beyond our imagining. At an international conference on how to spread the faith, many people suggested a media campaign on radio and TV. A young African delegate, however, suggested a different tack, offering a lesson learned in her country. If you want to convert a village, she said, don't send literature. Send a Christian family to live among them.

Many of us are discouraged by the seeming pervasiveness of evil in our world. In the first parable Jesus warned us it would always be such. We must have faith and patience. A story is told of a perspicacious Australian who felt that World War II was coming on and wanted to escape. He sought out the most remote, out of the way island he could find and moved there lock, stock and barrel. Unfortunately, the island he picked was Guadalcanal, which turned into one of the bloodiest, most prolonged battles of the war.

Buried Treasure, Pearl of Great Price

Today's Gospel contains four parables, the last of which is about the "scribe who is learned in the kingdom of God." We frequently hear about the scribes and Pharisees and their inveterate opposition to Jesus. I have talked about the Pharisees before. Today it might be good to say something about the scribes.

Scribes were people who studied the law and made their living transcribing it and interpreting it. Today we would call them lawyers. In ancient Palestine, however, all law derived from the Mosaic Law which was found in the Torah or first five books of the Old Testament. So the scribes were, in fact, experts in both religious and civil law, as well as being well versed in Scripture. They rose in prominence in Jewish history after the Exile when the law became a predominant force in Jewish life and culture. As that law became more complicated and convoluted under Pharisaical and rabbinical influence, people would go to the scribes for advice and interpretation of the law. Since the law was their living, they had perhaps an exaggerated respect for it and a stake in keeping it as obscure and arcane as possible. The easier the law became to understand and interpret, the less needed their services would eventually become. Jesus had in fact warned the ordinary people that, though the scribes had succeeded Moses as teachers and expositors of the law, they should not follow the scribes' example. The scribes in turn disliked Jesus because, though he was never formally educated as they had been in years of arduous schooling, he never hesitated to give his opinion or interpretation of the law. Worse, he was trying to make the law more accessible to the ordinary person and easier for everyone to follow and put into practice. This they may have interpreted as a threat to their livelihood and profession. Hence the strong dislike and opposition.

The first parable is about a buried treasure. While rare in our age and culture, a buried treasure was not uncommon in ancient

Palestine. There were no banks or safe deposit vaults at the time. Houses were relatively open because of the heat. The only really safe way to hide valuables was to bury them. When people died or were forced to flee for their lives, however, treasures were frequently lost or forgotten. If later uncovered, they belonged legally to whoever owned the land. The Parables of the Buried Treasure and Pearl are very similar in theme. While applicable to all, they had special urgency for the scribes. Both tell of something of inestimable value which is unexpectedly discovered and calls for immediate action lest a priceless opportunity be lost. The reign of God as announced by Jesus Christ is that something priceless, that buried treasure, that exquisite pearl, that people should give up all they own to possess. The scribes in particular who were educated in Scripture and the law should have appreciated the good news Jesus brought as the fulfillment of all the Old Testament prophecies and promises. They should have willingly sacrificed everything to obtain it and not have obstructed it or hindered it in any way.

The Parable of the Net is similar to last week's parable of the wheat and the weeds. The net is the kingdom of God which is open to all, the good and the evil, with the hope and expectation that the evil will repent and turn to good before the end. But in the event they fail to reform their lives, the contents of the net, the kingdom of God on earth, will be cleaned out in the end of time with the good separated from the evil, and the good rewarded while the evil are discarded, presumably into Gehenna.

The last parable refers to the scribes by name. "Every scribe who is learned is like the head of a household who can draw from his storeroom the new and the old." Here Jesus warns the scribes explicitly that if they wish to enter the kingdom of God, they must know how to draw upon the new revelation of Jesus as well as the ancient teachings and traditions of the law and the prophets. In effect, Jesus tells his Church, that there is not only continuity between his teaching and Old Testament revelation, but that he and his teaching are the fulfillment of all the Old Testament prophecies and expectations.

Multiplication of the Loaves

The multiplication of the loaves and fish is one of the best witnessed and most important miracles in the life of Jesus. It is the best witnessed because we are told it took place before and on behalf of more than 5000 people. We know it is extremely important because it is the only miracle Jesus performed that is recorded in all four Gospels.

The passage is rich is scriptural significance that looks both backward into history and forward into time. Today's account is from Matthew and Matthew, we recall, was eager to show his fellow Israelites that Jesus supersedes all the Old Testament personalities, even Moses, the greatest Old Testament teacher, leader, and law-giver. Before he died Moses asked God to send a new leader for the people so they would not be like sheep without a shepherd (Nb 27:16). When Jesus sees the people, he pities them for they were like sheep without a shepherd, suggesting he is Israel's new leader, Moses' successor. The miracle takes place around Passover time in a deserted place. The time of year in which the Jewish people celebrated their freedom from Egypt and the location of a deserted place would remind the Jewish audience of Moses who freed them from slavery and fed them with manna in the desert. Here they see Jesus free them from sickness and infirmities and feed them with bread and fish. Matthew is implying Jesus is greater than Moses.

In the Second Book of Kings (4:42) we read that when there was a famine in the land someone gave Elisha a few small loaves which he ordered his followers to distribute to a crowd of 100 men. Miraculously, the few loaves fed the 100 men. Here Jesus feeds more than 5000 people, indicating he has greater power than Elisha, one of the greatest Old Testament prophets and miracle workers.

Matthew also links the multiplication of the loaves to the death of John the Baptist. He does this by contrasting the miracle at which

Jesus feeds 5000 to the banquet at which Herod orders the behead-ing of John. The first half of chapter 14 in Matthew, is given over to the banquet at which Herod and his court selfishly enjoy them-selves with no concern for the welfare of others, not even their lives. By way of contrast, the multiplication of loaves and fish takes place precisely because Jesus is concerned by the plight of others and directs his Apostles to act to alleviate it. By means of this sharp contrast Matthew shows that Jesus is a compassionate leader, un-like Herod the temporal leader who as king was supposed to act as the shepherd of his people, Israel.

The miracle also looks forward to the future. It is a clear prefiguration of the Eucharist. We can see this from the marked similarity of the words used in this miracle to the words used in the institution of the Eucharist at the Last Supper. In all the accounts of the multiplication of loaves and fish, as well as in all the accounts of the institution of the Eucharist, we see virtually the same verbs and sequencing used. In Matthew's account of the multiplication, for instance, we read basically that Jesus took the loaves, blessed, broke, and gave them to the disciples. In Matthew's account of the institution of the Eucharist (26:26), we read that Jesus took the bread, blessed it, broke it, and gave it to the disciples. Making al-lowances for the fact that "bless" in Hebrew can also be translated "give thanks to God," it's the same sequence the priest uses each day at the consecration of the Mass: He took bread, blessed it / gave thanks, broke it, and gave it to his disciples.

The multiplication of the loaves and fish was intended to help the people accept the upcoming gift of the Eucharist. Jesus hoped that the many people who had seen him miraculously multiply bread physically, and the many more who later heard of it, would be bet-ter prepared to accept his word when he promised them bread that would help them live spiritually forever. The miracle was intended to show that if Jesus could multiply bread physically in a way no mere human could, then he could also change bread spiritually to feed us with his life forever.

The miracle of the loaves and fish has marvelous Old Testament connotations and rich Eucharistic overtones. But it also has practical implications. (1) Jesus clearly intended that his disciples be active in reaching out to help others. They were never to dismiss or ignore the needs of others. (2) Jesus made ample use of whatever they had or could muster. From five loaves and two fish he was able to feed over 5000 people. If we place ourselves and our talents at God's disposal, he too can work wonders through us.

I close with a story of Malcolm Muggeridge, a famous British TV commentator. A hardened atheist, Malcolm was sent to do a story on the work of Mother Teresa early in her career. Though cynical and skeptical at first, he was soon won over. He said he saw Christianity in action for the first time in his life and was so impressed by what one person could do, he decided to become a Catholic. He ended his account with a remarkable story. He wanted to film the nuns at work at a hostel for the dying. But it was a converted Hindu temple designed to keep out the heat, not let in the light. The camera crew had no lighting equipment and their film was only for bright sun. In desperation he ordered them to shoot anyway, hoping the film would at least capture shadows of the figures that could then be explained by his dialogue. When the film was developed, to everyone's amazement the nuns and patients could all be seen clearly, illuminated by an ethereal light emanating from the nuns. Unseen by the human eye, it was clearly discernible on the film. This was not the reason why Malcolm converted, however. He stoutly maintained it was due solely to the example of Mother Teresa and her love for others.

Jesus Walking on the Water

Today's account of Jesus walking on the water was very important and dear to the early Church. To see why, we should understand how it fits into the general structure of Matthew's Gospel and the overall significance of the sea to the early Jewish mind.

Let's start by fitting the passage into Matthew's Gospel. Matthew's account of Jesus' walking on the water comes shortly after the multiplication of the loaves and fish. This was Jesus' largest public miracle, but the crowds still proved more interested in a political rather than a spiritual Messiah. John (6:15) tells us they wanted to seize Jesus and make him king. So Jesus is forced to flee from them to preserve the integrity of his mission and from that moment on decides to concentrate more on forming the Apostles, less on reaching out to the crowds at large.

Jesus sends the Apostles on across the lake ahead of him and goes off by himself up a mountain to pray. In the Old Testament a mountain is usually the place for revelation and Jesus will soon make an astounding revelation. From his prayer on the mountaintop Jesus becomes aware that the Apostles are in distress and goes out across the lake to help them. The ensuing scene will be the first lesson directed solely at the Apostles, and notice how Peter is already being singled out.

To understand the significance of the episode to the contemporary Jews and early Christians, we have to understand the symbolism of the sea in the Old Testament. In Old Testament times the sea was commonly regarded as the dwelling place of the devil and his evil spirits. God inhabited the heavens; humankind, the earth; and the devil and his minions, the sea. It is easy to see how ancient people associated evil with the sea. The sea can rise up without warning, flood towns and villages, and send ships and sailors to a watery grave. Humankind was helpless before it and often

132

suffered terribly from it. It's no wonder it was considered a malevolent force. The Old Testament enforces the belief. Psalm 65, verse 8, tells us only God can control the sea. The Book of Genesis describes creation in part as God's personal victory over the sea. The creation account tells us that in the beginning the earth was a formless mass and there was darkness over the deep. God then sends his Spirit over the waters to calm them and begins creation, separating the waters and drawing forth land on which he continues the creation of everything good. In creating the universe, God is victorious over evil.

In today's Gospel Jesus is seen walking calmly on a turbulent sea. The event is clearly designed to show the Apostles that Jesus is God, with absolute power over the sea and hence all the forces of evil. As Job (9:8) tells us, "Only God can walk on the crest of a wave." The Apostles are terrified at the sight, however, and think at first it must be a ghost or some evil spirit. But Jesus calms them with the words, "It is I." The same words can also be translated "I am." It is from the Hebrew word "Yahweh," from which God's name is derived, and it is the exact same response that God gave to Moses when Moses asked God who he was. The response calms the Apostles and further strengthens the message that Jesus is truly God.

Peter is emboldened by the presence of Jesus and asks to come and join him. Jesus invites him and Peter steps out of the boat with confidence. But then he realizes where he is. His faith fails him and he begins to sink. When he calls on Jesus once again, however, he is rescued and brought back safely to the boat. The point Jesus makes here to Peter, the Apostles, and the early Church is that Peter too has power over evil, to walk on water and calm the raging sea. But that power, importantly enough, comes only through contact with and confidence in the person of Jesus. When Peter trusts, he can subdue the sea. When he doubts, he sinks and is lost. Thus the power to conquer evil, as manifested by subduing the sea, is not magical. It comes only through and with faith in Jesus.

From this incident the early Church took for itself what proved to be its favorite image: the Church as the bark of Peter. The Church regarded itself as the boat of Peter, with Peter at the helm, threatened by evil forces, such as the Roman Empire which persecuted it and sought to eradicate it, and Jewish religious authorities who wanted to stamp it out. But like the bark of Peter on a turbulent sea, the Church was confident that Jesus was near and if they trusted in him, they would be safe from all harm.

We can also draw comparisons to our own lives. Jesus first fed his disciples and then sent them off on their own. At Mass Jesus feeds us with the Eucharist and sends us off on our own to face the world. Like Peter's boat, we are often buffeted by pagan, hostile forces. Like Peter, we often fail to realize that Jesus, though unseen, is near. Though we often fail to notice, the risen Jesus also says to each one of us, "Have courage. It is I. I am with you." As long as Peter focuses on Jesus, he is safe. When he focuses on himself and his predicament, he sinks. This is just as true for us. If we place our trust in God and put ourselves at his disposal, God can do wonderful things through us. If we concentrate on ourselves and our own weaknesses, there is little we can do, especially in the work of God's kingdom.

So as we reflect on this Gospel, let us ask God to help us and the Church to be ever mindful of his presence and strength, to put our trust in him and not so much in ourselves.

The Canaanite Woman

Last Sunday we read about Jesus walking on the water and inviting Peter to do the same. This week we read about the Canaanite woman. Matthew wants to contrast the human behavior in both events and joins the two stories with an incident unfortunately omitted from the Sunday readings. The Pharisees had observed the Apostles eating with unwashed hands and complained to Jesus. Pharisees, which means "separated ones," kept their distance from any Jew who failed to observe the Mosaic Law and an even greater distance from Gentiles who knew neither God nor the law. The critical encounter between the Pharisees and Jesus over the importance of a minor purification rite sets the stage for the Canaanite woman, a Gentile and hence an outlaw to the Jews.

Today's Gospel is disturbing and confusing in terms of language and tone. Both are strikingly uncharacteristic of Jesus. Jesus, who has just been criticized by the Pharisees for not following tradition, now adheres strictly to tradition and refuses to speak to the woman. Jews were not supposed to speak to non-Jews; rabbis would not talk to a woman in public, even their wives. Recall when Jesus approached the Samaritan woman at the well and asked for water, it was she who was startled and wondered how it was that he, a Jew, would speak to her.

The Canaanite woman is persistent, however. Undeterred by his silence, she pleads again for help. Jesus replies even more uncharacteristically, using language offensive to us today but familiar at the time and commonplace among the Jews and rabbis. The Jews thought of themselves as God's children because they believed in the one true God and followed his laws. They also believed that non-Jews who did not acknowledge the one true God or follow his laws were less than human and no better than animals. And they did not hesitate to call them such, "dog" being the epithet of popular choice. So Jesus' reply, harsh as it seems, is exactly what the woman could expect from a Jewish rabbi. But Jesus was merely probing the depth of her faith. Amazingly, the woman turns the slur to her advantage, crying, "Even the dogs eat the scraps that fall from the table of their masters." Jesus responds, "Woman, great is your faith," and grants her request by immediately curing her daughter.

Matthew's presentation of the Canaanite woman thus reveals her as the female counterpart of the Roman centurion, also a pagan, of whom Jesus said, "I have not found such great faith in all of Israel." Ironically it is only in the pagan or Gentile world that Jesus has encountered people of truly deep faith. Notice, too, the striking contrasts. Matthew first contrasts the Canaanite woman with the scribes and Pharisees. She addresses Jesus with the Messianic titles, "Lord" and "Son of David," something the Jewish religious leaders were unwilling to concede. Matthew next contrasts the Canaanite woman to the Apostles. After being rebuffed the first time, she comes forward again and pays Jesus homage, a sign of worship, well before any miracle ever takes place. Earlier the Apostles had also paid Jesus homage, but only after they had witnessed his miraculous walking on the water. Lastly, Matthew contrasts the Canaanite woman to Peter himself. She, though a pagan, is called a "woman of great faith" shortly after Peter, the head of the Apostles, is rebuked as "one of little faith" for faltering as he walked towards Jesus on the water.

Today's Gospel marks the beginning of a major turning point in the ministry of Jesus. Up until this point in Matthew's Gospel Jesus has generally directed his efforts and mission to the lost sheep of the house of Israel. Moved by this woman's deep faith, however, he uses his miraculous power here on behalf of an outsider and accepts the profound reverence of a foreigner. Many see this event as the justification for Matthew's great commission at the end of his Gospel when Jesus tells the Apostles immediately before ascending into heaven: "Go, therefore, and make disciples of all the nations." It is ironic that Matthew, who stressed the primacy of

Jesus' mission to the Jewish people and saw the Church as the fulfillment of the Old Testament prophecies for Israel, is the only evangelist to include this commission in his Gospel and end it on such a universal note.

Though initially strange to Matthew, the notion of the universality of God's saving plan did not escape Isaiah. Second Isaiah (chapters 40-55) explained the Babylonian captivity to the exiles as part of God's plan to bring salvation to the Gentiles. He told them God would use them as instruments to bring other people to a knowledge and love of the one, true God. People in the areas to which they were exiled would witness their faith in Yahweh and come to worship God too. In today's first reading, Third Isaiah (chapters 56-66) also introduces a universal note. Unlike the prophet Ezekiel, who was known as the father of Judaism and adamantly opposed the presence of foreigners in the Temple, Third Isaiah welcomed all of good will to the Temple precincts. Writing after the return of the exiles from captivity and trying to encourage them to rebuild in face of hardships and the presence of the many foreigners who had settled in the area in their absence, Isaiah urges them to welcome all who come in sincere faith. He assures them in God's name that the sacrifices of anyone properly disposed will be acceptable and God's house will be a house of prayer for all peoples.

"You are Peter"

Today's Gospel took place at Caesarea Philippi, a city built by Herod the Great to the northeast of the Sea of Galilee in honor of the reigning Roman emperor. Herod's son Philip expanded the city and added his own name to it to distinguish it from the port city of Caesarea on the Mediterranean. It included a temple dedicated to Caesar Augustus whose massive statue Roman citizens and subjects were annually required to worship as a god. So when Peter is asked who Jesus is, he replies beautifully with the words, "You are the son of the *living* God."

Jesus praises Peter for his insight and changes his name. In ancient times a person's name was associated with his profession or call in life. We have vestiges of it today in names like Baker, Butcher, Taylor which originally identified the family's trade centuries ago. While changing names is not in vogue now, in Old Testament times God frequently changed the names of people when he gave them new assignments or missions. When God chose Abram to be the father of the Jewish people, he changed his name from Abram (the father is exalted) to Abraham (father of a host of nations). God also changed the name of Abraham's wife from Sarai to Sarah (princess), indicating her exalted status as the mother of the Jewish people. Later when God renewed the covenant with Abraham's grandson Jacob, he changed his name to Israel, which means "God is victor" or "God conquers," a name which the Jewish people later took for themselves, suggesting God had conquered them heart and soul and they wished to remain forever his people.

The name Jesus chooses for Peter is unusual. "Cephas" in Aramaic, "Petros" in Greek, means "Rock," and "Rock" or "Peter" had never been used as a name before. It was a popular symbol for God in the Old Testament, however. While not in vogue today, the Jews used "rock" as a symbol for God's strength, permanence, and im-

138

pregnability. To the ancient Israelites who had not mastered the skills of metallurgy, a rock was the strongest element they knew. Since God was strong, they called him a rock: the rock of Israel (Is 30:29), the rock of refuge (Is 17:10), and the rock of deliverance (Dt 32:15). In Palestine's hot humid climate, things decayed and rotted quickly. Only things of stone lasted for generations. For his timeless qualities, they also called God "rock." When the people made a covenant or pact with Yahweh, they frequently erected a pillar of stone called a stele and concluded with a prayer reminding the people that the stones had heard their promises and would stand as an everlasting witness to their pledge. It is the everlasting quality of a rock mentioned in Isaiah (26:4) that inspired the Anglican hymn, "Rock of Ages." A rock was also impregnable. A city with stone walls could not be taken. The one occupying the rocky heights was safe from attack. This is reflected in Psalm 18, verse 3, which inspired Luther's hymn, "A Mighty Fortress is our God."

More to the point, Isaiah referred to Abraham as the rock from which the Jewish people were hewn (Is 51:1). Following up on Isaiah 28, verse 16, which speaks of a stone that is laid as a cornerstone for a sure foundation, ancient homilies also refer to Abraham as the rock or cornerstone on which the Jewish people were founded. Jewish tradition also held that God placed a rock as the center of creation and then built the rest of creation upon it. "You are Rock and on this rock I shall build my Church," then, implies that Jesus is about to build a new people of God, his Church, on the foundation of Peter.

Jesus continues, "The gates of the nether world shall not prevail against it," the nether world being the abode of the dead. This suggests that Jesus will preserve the Church for all of time and it shall never cease to exist in the course of human history. "I entrust to you the keys of the kingdom of heaven." The significance of keys is illustrated in the first reading from Isaiah, chapter 22, which describes a transfer of the power of the Master of the Palace from Shebna to Eliakim. Shebna had abused his office as majordomo by siphoning off palace funds for his own use and so God gives the office to Eliakim. The Master of the Palace had the power to give or block access to the king, as symbolized by the keys he wore around his neck that opened or closed the gates to the palace. One could not get to the king without going through the Master of the Palace, much as one cannot get to the CEO without going through his executive secretary, so the role was crucial. As late as the Renaissance we see pictures of St. Thomas More, as Chancellor of the Realm, with the keys of the kingdom around his neck, indicating he had final say on who saw the king.

In giving Peter the keys of the kingdom of God, Jesus gives Peter the power to provide access to the Church, and through the Church to the kingdom of God, thus ultimately to God himself. This imagery is made even richer by Jesus' recent criticism of the scribes and Pharisees, accusing them of shutting off the kingdom of heaven from those who seek to enter. They did this by making the Mosaic Law too cumbersome and difficult for ordinary people to fulfill. By contrast Jesus reduces the many laws to two: love of God and love of neighbor and commissions the twelve to spread the good news.

In all three synoptic Gospels (Mt 16:13, Mk 8:27, Lk 9:18), Peter recognizes that Jesus is the Messiah. Peter is the divinely appointed head of the Church, and the Church will last forever through God's promise and protection. We sometimes have difficulties with the human administration of the Church, but we should always remember it is the Church Jesus founded and promised to be with until the end of time.

"Get Behind Me, Satan"

Today's Gospel is best seen in contrast to last week's Gospel. Last week Jesus asked Peter, "Who do people say that I am?" Peter replied, "You are the Christ, the Son of the living God." Jesus praised Peter for his response, changed his name from Simon to Peter, which means "rock," and made him the head of the Church, saying "You are Rock and on this rock I will build my Church." Peter's declaration, "Son of the living God," is a moment of exaltation for Jesus similar to the moment at his baptism when a voice from heaven declared, "This is my beloved Son in whom I am well pleased." And as the moment of exaltation in the baptism was followed immediately by a scene in which Jesus is tempted by the devil in the desert, so this moment of exaltation is also followed by a scene in which Jesus is once again tempted, but now by Peter, the head of his Church.

Having been declared the Christ or Messiah, Jesus goes on to describe the nature of his Messiahship. Jesus tells the Apostles for the first of three times that he must suffer and die. As newly appointed head of the Apostles, Peter objects out of love for Jesus and tries to dissuade him from such a course of action, saying, "God forbid, Lord! No such thing shall ever happen to you." And Jesus responds with an uncharacteristically strong and harsh rebuke. Jesus is upset because, though well intentioned, Peter is thinking by human standards and not by God's, and in so doing is unwittingly trying to get Jesus to circumvent the very essence of God's will and plan.

In the stinging rebuke Jesus directs at Peter, we see Peter suffer three reversals of fortune. (1) Last week Jesus called Simon "Rock," the foundation of his Church. This week, Jesus calls Peter "Satan," one set on destroying the Church. And Jesus gives to Peter the same command he gave Satan in the desert, "Away with you," or "Out of my sight." (2) Last week there was a play on words. Jesus changed Simon's name to Peter, which means "rock," and said, "On this rock, I will build my Church." This week we see another play on words. Our translation says, "You are an obstacle to me." The original says, "You are a *scandalon*," which means "a stumbling stone" or "a stumbling block." From the Greek word *scandalon,* we get the English word "scandal." The play on words shows the terrible reversal. Last week Peter was the cornerstone on which the Church is to be built; this week he is a stumbling stone interfering with God's plan.

The word *scandalon* also means "a stone used to drag fishing nets to the bottom of the sea." As a fisherman, Peter learns that his words act like a weight trying to drag Jesus down, away from God. *Scandalon* also meant "a trap or snare," and this also captures the meaning of Jesus' words and Peter's predicament.

The third reversal is found in the command, "Out of my sight." The original text has two verbs, "Get away," which Jesus used on Satan, and "Get behind me." Last week Jesus gave Peter the Primacy in the Church, making him first. This week Jesus puts him last, telling Peter to get behind him. But "Get behind me" can also mean "Follow me," and this softens the meaning. Jesus in effect tells Peter he is to lead the Church not by going off on his own, but rather by following in the footsteps of Jesus.

Having told Peter to get behind him physically, also implying he should follow him psychologically, Jesus invites us all to follow him and reminds us that we too must take up our cross — something that often strikes fear in our hearts and leads us to question the strength of our resolve. He also confronts us with the paradox that those who seek their life will lose it and those who lose their life will save it. It is often called the Christian paradox and unless and until we accept it, we are not thinking as God does.

It is easy to see it was true for Jesus. As Messiah, Jesus did not defeat the Romans as most of his contemporaries hoped he would. But in accepting death on the cross, he did defeat death itself. After his death, God raised him from the dead to eternal life. Death for Jesus, then, was not the end; it was the entrance to eternal life and happiness at God's right hand forever.

So, too, Jesus promises it will be for us. Those who give their lives to God will have eternal life with him forever. Those who live their lives for themselves will not. Paradoxically, the same is also true in this life. Those who make a career of seeking happiness rarely find it. The oft-tried paths to happiness — alcohol, drugs, promiscuity — are the surest and most direct routes to personal destruction and ruin. Those who think only of themselves end up with only themselves for company. The loving spouse, the devoted parent, the good friend obtains the joy of love not by grasping at it but by giving it generously at all costs.

Today's Gospel also marks a second call of the Apostles. Now that they know all that discipleship entails, Jesus invites them once again to follow him. It is a call to a more mature vocation. As Christians, we receive similar calls. Most of us were baptized as infants. When we are adults and the demands of the faith become more evident and arduous, we have continually to renew our commitment to follow Jesus and be his faithful disciples. The same is true in marriage or a vocation to religious life. Two people promise to love and honor each other when they are young. As they get older and change and things get more difficult, they have continually to renew their promise and commitment. It is part of any vocation.

"If Your Brother Sins Against You"

Today's Gospel comes from Matthew. In writing his Gospel, Matthew wanted to show his fellow Israelites that Jesus is truly the Messiah, the fulfillment of all the Old Testament prophecies. He is particularly fond of comparing Jesus to Moses, the greatest teacher, leader, and law-giver in the Old Testament. To Moses are attributed the first five books of the Old Testament, called the Pentateuch, Torah, or simply the Law. To highlight the similarity between Jesus and Moses, Matthew likewise divides his Gospel into five sections or books. Chapter 18, from which we read today, marks the beginning of the fourth book of Matthew. The fourth book of the Torah is called Numbers. Chapter 18 of Matthew is filled with numbers. In the passage immediately before today's we read of the 100 sheep, 1 of which is lost and 99 remain safe. In today's Gospel we read of 2 or 3 witnesses and 2 or 3 gathered together in prayer. Next week we will read of forgiving 70 x 7 times. All contain references to numbers.

Today's Gospel speaks about fraternal correction. Matthew uses "brother" to mean "a fellow member of the Church," so it refers to correcting a fellow Christian, even to the point of excommunication. But it is interesting that the passage is sandwiched in between two passages dealing with mercy. Just prior to this passage is the story of the one lost sheep and the shepherd leaving the 99 to find it. Right after this passage Jesus tells Peter he must be ready to forgive 70 x 7 times.

The unusual and seemingly contradictory juxtaposition of stories and messages, then, is but one indication that the Gospel message is complex. We can't take an isolated passage from Scripture and build our whole Christian life around it. We must see it as part of the Christian message and interpret it always in the context of the entire Bible and the whole Christian tradition. For example, if we were to read only today's section on excommunication, we might wrongfully conclude that all who disagree with us should simply be cut off and ignored. But in the context of the lost sheep that precedes it and the need to forgive 70 x 7 times that follows it, it is clear that our primary concern should be for reconciliation and pardon. It is only in cases of extreme recalcitrance and danger of harm to others that excommunication is called for.

Another naive extreme we need to avoid in interpreting Scripture is to read next week's passage of forgiving 70 x 7 times and conclude that we must forgive and forget no matter what. We must always forgive in the sense of never wishing the other ill, but we can never abrogate common sense. This would be to ignore today's Gospel which makes it clear that drastic measures are the appropriate Christian response if the person is recalcitrant and may harm another or the Church itself. The First Letter of St. Paul to the Corinthians (5:1) makes clear that there can be such cases. So while bending towards mercy, we must always have the steel to be strong when needed.

It is easy to see cases of both extremes about us. Generally speaking, we do not tend to be overly hard on others. But frequently we err by being overly hard on ourselves. We all know people who have given up on themselves long before exhausting the 70 x 7 rounds of forgiveness that Jesus speaks of, preferring to leave the Church or the Sacraments rather than presume on God's mercy and be hypocrites. It is often nobly intended but self-defeating and completely contrary to God's will. As the tale of the Lost Sheep shows, God's love for us is constant and far-reaching. It is not predicated on our strength or goodness.

The other extreme is mindless forgiveness in the sense of forgiveness without rationality. Several cases come to mind. Years ago, Norman Mailer pushed for the release of Jack Abbott, author of *In the Belly of the Beast*, arguing that such a brilliant author should not remain in prison despite the fact that the book lovingly portrays Abbott's stabbing a fellow inmate to death in prison. When released, Abbott got into an altercation with a 23-year-old bus boy at a restaurant, asked him to step outside, and proceeded to stab him to death exactly as he had described the stabbing of his fellow inmate in his book. A second case occurred at a mental hospital on Long Island. A young man was confined by the courts as a danger to his wife with the stipulation that the police and his wife be notified if he should ever be released. An intern concerned for patients' rights judged the warning harsh and unnecessary and released him on a weekend pass. The man then headed straight for home where he slit his wife's throat before their young children. Another more recent case is that of a man released from a mental hospital deemed cured of violence by medication but who refused to take his medication and pushed a young woman to death before a subway car. While we must always be ready to forgive, we can never abrogate reason or simple common sense and place our welfare and that of others in jeopardy.

God chose the image of a parent for himself in trying to explain his relationship to us, and perhaps a parent is the best illustration of what God intends by the balance between correcting and forgiving. Parents often have to exercise this type of tough love. They frequently have to reprove their children with words like, "Where do you think you're going in that outfit?" "You couldn't pay a maid to clean your room, and I'm no maid." "You're brother and sister, not cat and dog." "Stop feeling sorry for yourself and get on with your life." They do so out of love, risking seething resentment, but they do so for the good of the child. So should our correction of others be. May it always be out of love, and never out of pique or spite.

Forgive 70 x 7 Times

Today's Gospel comes at the end of an extensive teaching by Jesus on the theme of the need for mending interpersonal relationships and making them strong. Now Peter approaches Jesus and asks how many times he has to forgive. Rabbis had been asked this question from time immemorial and they generally agreed on three. After that they assumed, even God would not forgive. Peter knows that Jesus is generous and has come to bring the Old Testament law to fulfillment, so he goes farther, citing what to the Jewish mind was the perfect number, 7, and obviously believing that it was more than enough. But Jesus startles Peter with his answer. "No, Peter, not 7 times, but 70 x 7 times," which to the ancient Jewish mind was an impossibly large number.

The two numbers are also rich in Old Testament significance. In the Book of Genesis (4:15) after Cain killed his brother Abel, he knew the crime was so horrible it cried out for vengeance and asked God's mercy. To protect Cain, God put a mark on him and vowed that anyone taking vengeance on Cain or his offspring would pay sevenfold, an indefinitely large number. What was intended for protection soon was taken for privilege. Six generations later, Cain's descendant, Lamech, killed a man who injured him and a boy who struck him, and boasted anyone harming him would pay 70 x 7 times (Gn 4:24), an unfathomably large number. So by his careful choice of numbers, Jesus reverses the Old Testament trend towards vengeance and redirects it towards forgiveness.

To drive his point home, Jesus follows it up immediately with a parable. A parable is a story which compares an element in the audience with an element in the story, usually without the audience at first being aware of the comparison. A parable thus disarms the audience and allows them to absorb the story without becoming defensive. Only when the story is finished and the message has sunk in, does the point of the comparison become clear.

Here the story is about a servant who owed the king a huge amount of money. The original text says 10,000 talents. 10,000 was the largest number in the ancient scale of counting. From it we derive the English word "myriad." A talent was the largest denomination of money in the ancient world, equivalent to a $10,000 bill or whatever our largest bill happens to be. So 10,000 talents signifies an impossibly large sum, far greater than the total GDP of Palestine at the time which was about 600 talents. Thus it would take the whole economy of Palestine over 16 years to raise the equivalent of the debt. Or in microeconomic terms, a talent was worth 6000 denarii, a denarius being the equivalent of the daily wage. So 10,000 talents would take 60,000,000 days, or over 164,000 years, of work to pay off. An impossible task! Yet the king, who symbolizes God, forgives the debt completely and lets the servant go scot-free.

Having just been forgiven his debt, the servant meets another servant who owes him a much smaller amount. The original says a few denarii, a few days work. That servant pleads with him the same way he had pleaded with the king, but the servant who had just received mercy shows no mercy to his fellow servant. He has the man's whole family thrown into debtors' prison until they pay it back. Counterproductive though it seems today, in olden times people were imprisoned for defaulting on a debt, even though they could not hope to repay it from prison. The king is informed of this churlish behavior and immediately redresses the situation, to the detriment and utter ruin of the first servant.

When the parable is finished, the point of the parable becomes clear. Peter is being compared to the unjust servant because he wants to put a limit on forgiving others. And the message in turn applies to any of us who is unwilling to forgive. Unless we are willing to forgive others as our heavenly Father forgives us, 10,000 talents worth or without limit, God will not forgive us. As God has measured out to us, so must we measure out to others. It was a difficult reply for Peter to accept, but one he would be grateful for later on when out of weakness he cravenly denied Jesus three times and was desperately in need of forgiveness himself.

Tallulah Bankhead once said, "Getting old isn't for sissies." We might add, "Being Christian isn't for the fainthearted." Forgiveness doesn't come easily. It's hard for the human heart to forgive, especially when we have been hurt by someone we love. And it is often harder still to forget, to wipe the slate clean and simply let the whole thing pass. As the first reading from Sirach tells us, there is something in the human heart that likes to nurse a grudge, to mull over past hurts and injuries, real or imaginary, that we feel others have inflicted on us. Yet natural as the tendency is, it is clearly self-defeating and self-destructive. When we can't forgive and won't forget, we become very small, completely self-absorbed. We dry up inside and never have peace of mind. It's only when we let go of what's consuming us, only when we forgive and wipe the slate clean, that peace can return and we can get on with our lives.

Today's Gospel isn't easy. God wants us to love others as he loves them and to forgive them as readily and completely as he does. But it is hard to be as generous as God. Yet when we sin, we want God to forgive and forget. So, lest we be like the ungrateful servant who was forgiven much but wouldn't forgive in turn, let us pray that we also have the courage and magnanimity of heart to forgive and forget when others sin against us.

Those Hired Last

Have you ever heard of Dutch Schultz, a mobster during Prohibition? Dutch Schultz was the son of poor Jewish immigrants who found himself on the wrong side of the law at an early age. And from there things only got worse. Through a mixture of gall and brutality, including murder, he worked his way up to the top as a prominent mob leader during Prohibition. He died as he had lived, in a hale of bullets, as he emerged from a restaurant. But before he expired, he was taken to a hospital where a priest came to him and explained the tenets of the faith. Dutch Schultz repented of his sins and asked to be baptized. The priest baptized him immediately and soon after he died.

Catholic teaching holds that anyone who dies immediately after Baptism goes straight to heaven. But instead of joy in the Church that a sinner had been saved, there was a public outcry. People were outraged that a man who had spent his life in crime and was a self-admitted multiple murderer should go scot-free into heaven when they had to toe the line and keep the Commandments all their life long. It seemed totally unfair and led many to question the justice of God. While understandable from a human point of view, however, it was far from Christian. Jesus tells us to rejoice at the conversion of a sinner and never to be jealous of God's love for others.

This selfsame attitude existed in the time of Jesus, as seen so often in the Pharisees. The Pharisees, remember, dedicated themselves to the perfect observance of the Mosaic Law. They were openly hostile to Jesus because of his attitude towards sinners and tax collectors. They objected to his willingness to forgive them and welcome them into the kingdom of God as the equals of themselves, who had rigorously kept the Mosaic Law all their lives. Worse, they objected to his opening of the kingdom of God to non-Jews who had never even heard of the Mosaic Law. The Pharisees felt they had earned God's love by their observance of the Mosaic Law and it was unfair of God to allow others such as sinners or Gentiles, who either flouted God's law or were ignorant of it, to share in the same rewards. They acted as if God owed them something and should be indebted to them for their goodness.

Jesus proposes this parable, then, to strike down this self-righteous attitude and show that God's love is more magnanimous than humankind can ever imagine. God's sense of justice, it turns out, is far more merciful than mankind's and is in no way unfair. Still the parable can be confusing and people often end up siding with the laborers rather than the landlord. So let's try a similar parable to clear things up. Say the country is in the midst of an economic downturn and two of your brothers with families to support are out of work. Neither qualifies for welfare or unemployment benefits. You have a small business which is struggling. You don't need any help, but by stretching you can hire one of your brothers, but in no way both of them. So you hire one, who works hard all week and on Sunday you invite both brothers and their families for dinner. At the end of the meal you hand the one who worked a fair salary and out of charity give an equal amount to the other from your savings. Would the first brother who worked all week have the right to complain? Would he be justified in demanding more from you because he had worked and the other had not? Surely not. You are being generous to both siblings and in no way cheating or being unfair to either. The point of the parable, then, is that salvation is a gift from God freely bestowed. We are asked to cooperate with God but it is never something we earn independently or on our own merits. If you look at the story carefully, you will notice that the laborers never complain about the wage they freely agree to, so it is not a question of justice. They complain only when they see others getting the same wage. Consequently, it is a matter of jealousy.

Equally important is the question, who received the greater gift? The ones who didn't work and got paid or the ones who worked and got the same pay? When you think of it, it's the ones who worked who were more blessed. In ancient Palestine daily laborers lived from hand to mouth and had to use one day's wage to pay for the next day's food. There was no surplus, no savings. If they didn't work one day, their families didn't eat the next day. Those who were hired early, therefore, even though they had to work a full day, had the assurance all day long that their families would eat the next day; those hired late, did not. Therefore, those hired early had even more reason to be grateful, and no reason to complain.

Finally, the question of the wage. Perhaps the owner could have given those who worked a full day a little more. But the wage is being compared to entrance into the kingdom of heaven, and there is no reward greater than that. God is offering us an inestimable gift. There's nothing greater he can give. And his love is so great, there is no way he is willing to give less to those who sign on late.

So as we reflect on the parable, let us be grateful that God has loved us so much that he freely invites us to share his life with him in heaven forever. Let us also ask for a share of his generosity of spirit so we too can rejoice when others are called to share that joy with us, even if, humanly speaking, they might not seem to deserve it. And let us also pray for the wisdom to realize that we who have been called early, most of us from birth, have been the most highly blessed because we have the comfort and security all our lives long of knowing that God loves us and has prepared a place for us that we will enjoy forever if we but follow his call and cooperate with his grace.

The Parable of the Two Sons

Today's Gospel from Matthew is the first of three parables that Jesus directs at the chief priests and elders. To understand today's parable, we have to go back a little farther in the Gospel. As Jesus entered the Temple area, the chief priests and elders who were in charge of the Temple came up to confront him. They asked by what authority Jesus did the things he was doing, namely, healing the sick and teaching with authority. Jesus recognized at once that they were trying to trap him. If he answered "by divine authority," they would accuse him of blasphemy. If he said "by my own authority," they would accuse him of over-stepping his bounds and interfering in their sphere of religious leadership.

Because of their evil intentions Jesus uncharacteristically decides to turn the tables on them and give them a taste of their own medicine. He tells them he will answer their question only if they answer his. And the question he asks, though simple and straightforward, traps them and places them on the horns of a dilemma. "Was the mission of John the Baptist of divine or human origin?" If they said "of divine origin," they would convict themselves of failing to heed God's message and messenger, since John had pointed out Jesus as the Lamb of God and directed his disciples to follow him. And if they said "of human origin," they would look foolish, for even the ordinary people could see that John was truly a great prophet.

To escape the dilemma, they simply refuse to answer. So Jesus proposes a parable, aimed straight at them and intended to call them to conversion. Remember, a parable is a story in which an element in the story is compared to the audience, without the audience at first being aware of the comparison. Jesus used the device to keep them from putting up defenses. By casting the story in terms of neutral third parties, the audience could listen to the story objectively, draw conclusions from the story without prejudice, and form unbiased judgments about the characters in the story without feeling threatened. Then when they had drawn their conclusions, often correctly, and the point of the story started to sink in, they finally realized it was about them.

Today's parable, the shortest in the whole Gospel, is cast simply in terms of two sons. The father approaches one son and asks him to work in his vineyard. The son refuses and walks away but later thinks the better of it and goes to the vineyard to work. The father goes to the other son and likewise asks him to work in his vineyard. The second son says yes immediately but then simply never bothers to go. Though neither son is a prize and both leave a lot to be desired, Jesus asks the chief priests and elders which of the two sons did the father's will. And the chief priests and elders answer correctly, "the first son," the one who eventually did what the father asked of him.

Then Jesus reveals the point of the parable by telling the chief priests and elders that tax collectors and prostitutes will get into the kingdom of heaven before they do. It is only then that they realize they have been compared to the second son in the story, the one who initially said he would do the father's will but then failed to deliver on his commitment. The chief priests and elders had initially said yes to God and had adjusted their lives to conform with the revelation that had come down from Moses and the prophets. But then when God sent his Son to bring the fullness of revelation and call them to an even closer relationship, they refused to accept the invitation and preferred to stay locked in their old familiar ways. They were like the second son in paying God lip service and then refusing to put his will into practice. They were blocking God's initiative by refusing to accept his Son, Jesus Christ.

It is to tax collectors and prostitutes, the most flagrant and notorious sinners of the day, that Jesus compares the first son, the one who first refused but then ultimately did the father's will. Sinners, as symbolized by tax collectors and prostitutes, also refused to do God's will at first and flouted his law by the lives they led, but many of them ultimately repented at the preaching of John the Baptist, changed their lives, and turned to follow Jesus. Jesus thus indicates that God prefers the humble who realize their mistakes and seek to correct them to the proud of heart who will not accept God's initiative in their lives.

The first reading from Ezekiel has much the same meaning as the parable. Royal officials earlier complained to Ezekiel that God was unfair and was punishing the current generation for the sins of their fathers. "The fathers have eaten sour grapes and the children's teeth are set on edge." Ezekiel answers that God's ways are not unfair. God does not judge people for the sins of their ancestors, he judges them on their own merits or lack thereof. Life is not a balance sheet in which more good years than bad years add up to heaven and the reverse to hell. God is so loving and willing to forgive that he will forgive anyone who repents even after a life of sin. But God will not force the human will. If, after a good life, a person turns against God and refuses to repent, God cannot force the human heart to change and it is the individual who must bear the responsibility for his actions and take the consequences. While God's love and support are always there for us and he always invites all sinners to repent, the passage is a reminder that we cannot rest on our laurels and assume that a good life in the past will save us. As children of God, we must continue to grow in the love of the Lord each and every day and keep that love relationship alive and strong.

Parable of the Vineyard Owner

The readings for today's liturgy are particularly beautiful. Three of the four are about a vineyard. A vineyard was very important to ancient people and so God used it frequently as a symbol for Israel, his chosen people. A vineyard was important in ancient Palestine because it provided grapes which were a succulent fruit in the heat of summer and, when dried as raisins, a sweet treat in winter when other fruits were not generally available. Even more importantly, at a time before painkillers, tranquilizers, and sedatives, it provided wine, which was a major source of relaxation and merriment for ancient people. A vineyard, then, was understandably an individual's prized possession and that is why God used the image of a vineyard in Scripture to symbolize his love for his people. Just as ancient people loved and cared for their vineyards, so God loved and cared for Israel. And just as the fruit of the vine gave joy to the human soul, so the fruit of human endeavor gave joy to God.

The first reading from Isaiah is called the "Song of the Vineyard" because Isaiah wrote it in the form of a ballad that could be sung. It is also like a parable. A parable is a story which compares the audience to an element in the story without the audience at first being aware of the comparison. In this song Isaiah's friend is God himself and the vineyard stands for Israel. Isaiah's friend picked the very best spot for his vineyard, carefully prepared the soil, selected the best vines, and carefully nurtured his crop. But instead of good fruit, the vineyard produced wild grapes which were small and sour, unsuitable for eating and unfit for wine. In disgust the owner decides to tear down the vineyard and plant another. Up until now the audience is all with the owner. But then Isaiah reveals the point of the parable. They, the Jewish people, are the vineyard and they have failed to bear good fruit. Fruit, remember, was used in Scripture to symbolize good works. We see this in the last two stanzas where the owner says, "I looked for justice and judgment but found only bloodshed and outcries," that is, oppression of the poor.

Psalm 80 also speaks of a vineyard as a symbol for Israel. It was written after the conquest of the Northern Kingdom by Assyria in 721 BC. In it the psalmist asks why God allowed his chosen vineyard, Israel, to be destroyed. He recalls how God had transplanted the vine (Israel) from Egypt and had driven out other nations (from the Holy Land) to plant Israel securely, how he then nurtured it until it had spread as far as the (Mediterranean) sea, its western border, and the (Euphrates) river, which was actually far beyond its eastern border. Why then, he now asks, after so much effort on Israel's behalf, did God allow his vineyard, the nation, to be destroyed and laid waste? He answers his own question, acknowledging that their own sins have led to their destruction, and concludes by asking that Israel be restored, promising they will not sin again.

The Gospel reading is also a parable of a vineyard, this time aimed at the chief priests and elders who are at first unaware that the parable is being directed at them. Jesus tells an engrossing story of a man who leases his vineyard to tenant farmers and goes off on a journey. At vintage time, he sends servants to collect his share of the harvest. But the tenants are not of a mind to pay, and they maltreat the servants. A second time the owner sends even more servants to collect what is due him. Again the tenants refuse to pay and abuse the servants. Finally the owner sends his only son to collect his rent, in the belief that the tenants will respect his son. But the tenants decide to kill the son so there will be no one to inherit the vineyard they have usurped. They drag the son out of the vineyard and kill him. Jesus then asks the unsuspecting chief priests and elders what the owner should do. They reply indignantly and self-righteously that the owner should take the vineyard from the tenants and give it to others. It is only then, after they condemn themselves, that Jesus reveals that they, as the religious leaders of the Jewish people, are the evil tenant farmers who did not manage the vineyard, Israel, well.

This parable is unusual in that it was turned into an allegory by the early Church. A parable generally has only a single point of comparison. An allegory, on the other hand, is a tale in which all the elements of the story have a specific point of comparison. While Jesus most probably delivered the parable as a warning to the religious leaders, the early Church saw rich symbolism in the story and developed it in its oral tradition. Hence we see the vineyard symbolizing the Jewish people. The owner is God. The tenant farmers are the religious leaders responsible for nurturing the Jewish people. The first group of servants are the prophets sent before the Exile, many of whom were maltreated by the religious leaders. The second group of servants were the prophets sent after the Exile, many of whom were also badly treated, some of whom were killed, and one of whom, Zechariah, was stoned to death in the court of the Temple itself. The son is Jesus and just as the owner's son was taken outside of the vineyard and killed, so Jesus was taken outside the city walls to a place called Golgotha where he was publicly executed on the cross.

Today's readings show God's tremendous love for us. The image of the vineyard shows how important his people are to him and how much effort he has extended in making us fruitful. But history shows humankind often fails to respond to God's love. So let us pray that we truly bear good fruit in showing love for one another and striving to be pleasing to God in all we do.

Parable of the Wedding Feast

Today's Gospel joins together two parables about a wedding feast. To understand the first, we need to set it in a scriptural and historical context. From a scriptural point of view, we should recall that all through Scripture God compared heaven to a wedding feast because nothing delights the human heart more than to sit down at table with those we love. The Jewish people regarded God's covenant with them on Mount Sinai as a wedding between God and Israel. They also looked forward to the coming of the Messiah as a time when God would renew his wedding covenant with his people and there would be joy and plenty as at a wedding feast. So when we hear of an invitation to a wedding feast, we should think automatically of an invitation to God's kingdom, heaven.

From a historical point of view, we should also recall that preparing a king's wedding feast took a considerable amount of time. An exact date could not be given. It was usually scheduled for the end of harvest time when the storehouses would be brimming. Guests were given the approximate date well in advance and then expected to keep the time free until an exact date could be fixed. Imagine then how the king must have felt in a culture particularly sensitive to honor and shame when, after the first warning, no one kept the date free and no one bothered to show up for his son's wedding. The story is clearly designed and set forth to show the king's largesse in inviting his subjects and his subjects' churlishness and callousness in rejecting the invitation.

The story, as Jesus told it and as Luke records it, was most probably a parable, that is, a story in which there is only one point of comparison, in this case aimed directly at the chief priests and elders. They had accepted God's initial invitation at Sinai and given their allegiance to the one true God. But when God invited them to an even deeper relationship through his Son Jesus, the promised

Messiah, they refused to follow. The point of the original parable, as seen in Luke's simpler version of the story, was that since they, the religious leaders, now refused to accept God's gracious invitation, that invitation would be withdrawn from them and given to others. In Luke's account, the dignitaries who were invited first are simply excluded from the banquet, not killed; and their places, filled by ordinary folk.

Over time, however, as this story was passed along by word of mouth in the oral tradition, the early Church began to notice many rich symbols and prophetic insights which they proceeded to bring to the fore in its retelling. In so doing the early Church changed what was originally a parable with a single meaning into an allegory with many meanings. And it is this allegorical version that Matthew eventually wrote down some fifty years later and which we read today. From the hindsight of history, Matthew's Gospel suggests that the wedding invitation is an invitation to the kingdom of God. God the Father is the one who gives the banquet. Jesus is the Son for whom the banquet is given. The servants God sends twice are the prophets, one group before the Babylonian Exile; the other group, after the Exile. Those who were invited first but refused to come are the chief priests and elders, the same group who also refused to heed the prophets and often maltreated them. Writing after the destruction of Jerusalem by the Romans in 70 AD, Matthew incorporates history into his Gospel and makes clear that the punishment for those who refused God's invitation included destruction of their city. Those who are subsequently invited to fill up the banquet hall include sinners and Gentiles or non-Jews, a sign once again of God's largesse, indicating that God wishes everyone to be saved.

The second parable is about the guest who came in without a wedding garment. Upon the refusal of the original guests, the Jewish leaders, the king sends out a third group of servants, the Apostles, to invite everyone they meet, suggesting once again the universality of God's love and kingdom. But one of those so invited comes in without a wedding garment and is thrown out into the darkness. This at first glance is disturbing because we wonder how someone invited late can be expected to have a wedding garment. The answer is that the wedding garment is being used symbolically. Clothing is often used as a symbol for conduct. A nurse who is capped accepts the responsibility of caring for her patients. A person wearing an army uniform is expected to act according to the military code of conduct. The same holds true for a policeman, a priest, or a nun. In Baptism a white cloth is placed on the child with the words, "Put on the garment of Christ," meaning "live your life in a manner befitting your new status as a child of God." The guest without a wedding garment, then, is simply a symbol for one who did not put on the conduct of Christ, one who did not repent of his sins and take on the love of God.

The second parable is a reminder that many are called, but few are chosen. It is not enough simply to receive God's invitation. We all receive God's gracious invitation. To be saved, to gain entrance into God's kingdom, we must follow through on the invitation, change our lives, and live truly as children of God.

Render to Caesar

There's a lot more going on in today's Gospel than at first meets the eye. Matthew clues us in from the very beginning by telling us that the Pharisees and Herodians were trying to entrap Jesus. "Entrap" is an unusual word. This is the only time it is used in all the Gospels and Matthew uses it deliberately because it was against Jewish law to entrap any human being. The Pharisees and Herodians whom we see conspiring together against Jesus were bitter enemies and so very unusual allies. The Pharisees were religious zealots. They strove to observe the Mosaic Law perfectly. They were also ardent nationalists who wanted complete independence for the Jewish people. The Herodians on the other hand were avowed secularists and unabashed Roman sympathizers. They cared not a whit about God or religion and openly collaborated with Rome. The Pharisees wanted to depose Rome; the Herodians sought to promote Rome.

If we look at the Pharisees first, we see that the Pharisees opposed Rome for religious and political reasons. From a religious point of view, the Torah held that Israel was a theocracy. A theocracy is a people ruled by God, just as a democracy is a people ruled by the people. The early Jews believed that God alone was their king and they later accepted a human king only on the condition that he serve as an envoy of God. The Pharisees therefore regarded Caesar as a usurper of God's rightful place and prerogatives and wanted to be rid of him. They also opposed Rome for its taxation policies on religious grounds. Roman taxes could only be paid in Roman coins and Roman coins were engraved with the image of Caesar. As religious Jews, they considered all graven images a form of idolatry. Even today, for instance, Orthodox Jews never allow photographs to be taken for fear of idolatry. To compound matters,

Roman coins also bore the inscription: "Tiberius Caesar son of the divine Augustus."

From a political viewpoint, the Pharisees objected to Roman rule and domination for nationalistic reasons. They opposed paying tax to support a government that had conquered them and subjugated them by force. When Pompey captured Jerusalem in 63 BC, he levied an excessively brutal tax to punish the hostile citizenry. Julius Caesar, a more seasoned diplomat, later eased the taxes and allowed a tax holiday every seven years when the Jews observed a sabbatical year. A sabbatical year was a time in which no crops could be planted in order to allow the soil time to renew itself. It was consequently also a time in which no income was generated. Nevertheless taxes are always hated and the Jews faced the equivalent of federal, state, and city taxes. The Romans taxed individuals, land, harbors, and imports; regional officials taxed crops and local production; city officials, anything passing through the city gates.

Taxes in Palestine were also hated because of the way they were collected. The Romans set the minimum they wanted to collect from each locality and then leased out the task of actually collecting the taxes to the highest bidder. It was up to the one getting the contract to collect enough to cover what the Romans expected plus a surplus to cover his own expenses and provide him with a comfortable profit. Those attracted to such a business tended to be an unscrupulous and unmerciful lot and the ordinary people despised them both for their greed and their collaboration with Rome.

The Herodians, on the other hand, the other party to the plot, were politicians and allies of Herod who supported Rome and profited from their Roman connections. They had no interest in religion or nationalism, and wanted only wealth and power. Since the best way to get ahead in the Roman Empire was to curry favor with Rome, they freely collaborated with Rome. The only thing holding the Pharisees and Herodians together was their mutual hatred of Jesus, exemplifying: "My enemy's enemy is my friend."

The Pharisees and Herodians thought they had Jesus in an impossible bind. If he says it is lawful to pay tax to Caesar, the Pharisees would report to the people he was breaking Mosaic Law, collaborating with the pagan Roman Empire, and even supporting emperor worship. If he answers no, the Herodians would report to the Romans that Jesus was breaking civil law and stirring up unrest.

Jesus masterfully escapes this seemingly inescapable dilemma by simply asking for a coin. In doing so, he indicates that he carries no Roman coins and so is not committing any idolatrous act or abetting the Roman system. When his opponents dig into their pockets and pull out a Roman coin, however, they expose their own hypocrisy. They are carrying about in their own pockets the very engraved images they claim to be idolatrous. And in so doing they are participating in the Roman system they allege is oppressive. In reminding them to "Render to Caesar the things that are Caesar's," Jesus subtly yet pointedly reminds them that if they are benefiting from the advantages that Rome brings, such as international peace, an unparalleled road system, expanded commerce, up-to-date communications, and a currency that was stable and universally accepted around the world, then they should also pay their fair share of the taxes.

In reminding them to "Render to God the things that are God's," Jesus also reminds them of their hypocrisy before God. The Pharisees claim to be loyal followers of God, but they refuse to accept the continuation of revelation that God is making known to them in the person of his Son, Jesus Christ.

The Greatest Commandment

In this section of Matthew's Gospel, we see the Sadducees and Pharisees united in a joint effort to trap Jesus. Their alliance is extremely unusual because they were situated at opposite ends of the political and religious spectrum and bitterly opposed to each other. The Sadducees were the priestly class who were liberal and largely secular in their outlook. In charge of the Temple, they worried more about the money it brought in than the worship it offered to God. We see a result of their evil stewardship later in the Gospel when Jesus has to purify the Temple. They also abetted the Roman regime to protect their interest in the Temple. In short, they cared more about Caesar than God. The Pharisees, on the other hand, were mostly lay people, many of them lawyers, who were religious zealots. They dedicated themselves to the perfect observance of the Mosaic Law and wanted to be rid of Roman domination. It was only their mutual hatred of Jesus that let them put enmity aside and band together to bring down Jesus.

In the passage immediately before this, the Sadducees tried to trip Jesus up on the notion of resurrection, which they, though priests, did not accept. But Jesus proved too much for them. In today's Gospel it is the Pharisees' turn and they hone in on the Law. In biblical times, law meant the Mosaic Law. The Mosaic Law is contained in the first five books of the Old Testament which were generally attributed to Moses himself and regarded as the most sacred of all the Old Testament. Collectively they are called the Torah which means simply the Law. In the Torah or Law attributed to Moses, there are 613 different commands: 248 positive, you-shall commands; and 365 negative, you-shall-not commands. The Ten Commandments which we revere are but a small part of these 613 precepts. For a population that was largely illiterate, the 613 precepts were more than most people could ever learn or remember, let alone put into practice.

Yet it was common belief that salvation depended on the fulfillment of the Mosaic Law. So you can see the bind the ordinary person was in. How could one fulfill the Law if one could not possibly learn or remember all of the law's many precepts? Some, like the moderate rabbis and the liberal Sadducees felt distinctions had to be made between grave and less grave commandments, as Catholics distinguish between mortal and venial sins; but others, like the Pharisees, held that all 613 precepts were of equal importance and all 613 had to be observed perfectly to fulfill the Mosaic Law and achieve salvation. This is why Jesus will later condemn the Pharisees for putting impossible burdens on other people's shoulders.

So it was not an innocent question the Pharisees asked Jesus. It was a hotly debated issue, particularly in the two centuries preceding the birth of Christ when the Pharisees flourished. Even the moderates who felt some distinctions had to be made among the many commandments could not agree on which were important and which were not, much less on which was the greatest commandment of all. The Pharisees and Sadducees, therefore, thought they had Jesus in a trap. If he picked one commandment from the rest as the greatest, the Pharisees would accuse him of downgrading the overall Torah which was Moses' final teaching and legacy. If he replied that all were of equal importance, the Sadducees would argue he lacked common sense and was placing the ordinary person in an impossible bind.

Jesus escapes brilliantly, however, with not one but two commandments from the Torah. The first is from Deuteronomy: "You shall love the Lord your God with all your heart, with all your soul, and with all your mind." The second is from Leviticus: "You shall love your neighbor as yourself." By making a distinction, Jesus offers no offense to the Sadducees who felt a hierarchy was necessary. And by picking two that are clearly all-inclusive of the others, he gave no reason for offense to the Pharisees either. Jesus clearly shows his genius, as no one before him had ever been able to do, by cutting through the multitude of laws that made life difficult for ordinary people and exposing the core on which all of the law depends. For if we truly love God above all things, we will do nothing willingly to offend him and so will keep all the laws directed towards God. And if we truly love our neighbors, we will do nothing willingly to offend them. In so doing, we will keep all of the other commandments, which are directed towards our neighbor.

As a good teacher, Jesus also made it easier for people to remember. The first precept comes from Deuteronomy, chapter 6, verse 5, and was one of the favorite passages in the Old Testament. Devout Jews recited it as their morning and evening prayer. Known as the *Shema* from the Hebrew word for "hear," it reads "Hear O Israel, Yahweh your God is the only God. You shall love the Lord your God with all your heart, with all your soul, and with all your mind." So Jesus simply reminds people to put into practice what most of them pray each day. The second, "Love your neighbor as yourself," also sums up and sets the tone for all our dealings with each other. Later Jesus will take this commandment beyond Old Testament morality where "neighbor" was taken to mean "fellow Jew." In the Parable of the Good Samaritan, Jesus will show that the neighbor can be a Samaritan, a member of a despised class, indicating we must love not only our own kind, but all God's children of every race, color, and creed.

In sum, at a time when religion was multiplying commands and the requirements for salvation, making life more difficult for the ordinary person, Jesus simplified it and put it within everyone's grasp. If we simply love God and neighbor, we will fulfill all of God's commandments.

Scribes and Pharisees

In today's Gospel Jesus speaks of the scribes and Pharisees in unusually harsh terms. In doing so he reveals a fundamental difference between himself and them. Last week Jesus took the whole Mosaic Law, all 613 different precepts of it, and summed it all up in two commandments: love of God and love of neighbor. He told us if we truly love God and if we truly love our neighbor, then we will be keeping all the commandments. The scribes and Pharisees held a very different view, however.

The scribes were experts in the Mosaic Law. They earned their living transcribing Scripture from scroll to scroll and used the knowledge they acquired in the transcriptions to act as lawyers for a population that was largely illiterate. In those days all law, civic and religious, emanated from the Mosaic Law which is found in the Torah. Hence the scribes were called upon to serve as legal advisers in areas both temporal and spiritual. Part of the problem stemmed from the fact that much of the Mosaic Law was couched in general principles. Let us look at the Ten Commandments with which we are most familiar and recall that they are only 10 of the 613 precepts in the Mosaic Law. The third Commandment, for instance, says "keep holy the Sabbath." But what does that mean? People generally want to know precisely what they can do and what they can't do. So the scribes, as lawyers, set out to pinpoint precisely what each precept meant and this led to unfortunate and unending distinctions which simply multiplied the laws.

Keeping holy the Sabbath, they concluded, meant many things. To cite a single example, no servile work. Fine. But what is servile work? Servile work, they found, also meant many things. One thing it meant, for example, was not walking too far because distance could change the nature of the action from recreation to work. Fine. But how far is too far and does one's motivation make a difference, as in the case of one's going to help someone in need? Each of these distinctions added to the number of laws. They were eventually codified in what is now known as the Talmud, which runs scores of volumes, making it impossible for people to remember all the laws, let alone put them into practice.

The Pharisees were close allies of the scribes. The Pharisees, whose name means "the separated ones," were a group of lay people who dedicated themselves to the perfect fulfillment of the Mosaic Law. Some 200 years before Christ when many Jews were adopting secular ways under Antiochus IV, the Pharisees bucked the trend. They were originally well-intentioned, but soon grew excessively legalistic, overly harsh, and self-absorbed. They insisted that all 613 precepts of the Mosaic Law and all the man-made additions of the Talmud had to be observed perfectly. Jesus called this an impossible burden. Even their peers found them too much. William Barclay lists seven categories of Pharisees found in the Talmud, only one of which is favorable. (1) Shoulder Pharisee: one who wore all his good deeds on his shoulder to be seen; (2) Wait-a-Little Pharisee: one who always had an excuse for putting off a good deed; (3) Bruised Pharisee: one who walked into walls because he kept his eyes closed to avoid seeing women; (4) Hunchbacked Pharisee: one who bent over to appear pious; (5) Ever-calculating Pharisee: the kind who was always adding up his good deeds; (6) Timid Pharisee: one always in fear God would punish him; (7) God-loving Pharisee: the type who was happy to keep the Law and walk in God's way (*The Gospel of Matthew*, Vol. 2, pp. 283-284).

With this as a background, we can see why Jesus tells the people to obey the scribes and Pharisees when they hand on the God-given laws contained in the first five books of the Old Testament, but to ignore their example and their exaggeration of the man-made precepts outside the Torah. Jesus also objects to their love of show. The Book of Deuteronomy directs people at prayer to wear phylacteries on their foreheads and wrists. Phylacteries were little boxes containing four of the most sacred passages in the Old Testament: (1) Exodus 13:1-10: Mazzoth Torah: about the first-born being consecrated to God; (2) Exodus 13:11-16: Passover Torah: also about the first-born being consecrated to God; (3) Deuteronomy 6:4-9: the *Shema*: "Hear O Israel"; (4) Deuteronomy 11:13-21: "There shall be no false gods." The same four quotations are also found in the Mezuzah, the plaque pious Jewish families place on the lintels of their doors. Wearing these quotations on their forehead signified they were to be the motivating reason for all their actions; wearing them on the wrist, that they might put into practice what God wanted. The Pharisees exaggerated the size of these phylacteries as they did all signs of devotion to call attention to themselves. They also lengthened their prayer shawl tassels, which were reminders of the precepts of the law. In short, they were often more interested in externalizing religion than internalizing it.

Jesus also criticizes them for seeking signs of honor like front seats in synagogues and banquets and titles of respect such as teacher, father, and rabbi. In ancient times, teacher, father, and rabbi were all titles of great respect. Jesus objects to the desire for praise that seeks such titles and he employs hyperbole to reject it. He says that we are to call no one "teacher," though we have all had many teachers. He simply means no human teacher compares to him. Teachers teach us how to live on earth. Jesus teaches us how to live for eternal life in heaven. Jesus exaggerates again and tells us to call no one "father" though we clearly all have biological fathers. He simply means human fathers pale before God. Human fathers give us human life; God gives us eternal life.

Jesus ends with a play on words in the title, rabbi. "Rabbi" means literally "great one," but is usually translated "teacher" or "master." The scribes and Pharisees craved being called "rabbi" or "great one." But Jesus declares the greatest among us is the one who serves the needs of all, not the one who is served by others as the Pharisees wanted. In doing so Jesus reverses the accepted order of the ancient world. He tells us if we truly wish to be great and achieve honor in God's sight, we must serve the needs of all by loving all people as God loves them. So let us pray that we have the humble, generous spirit Jesus proposes for us today and recall to our edification that the popes have always signed their letters "the servant of the servants of God."

The Ten Bridesmaids

Today's Gospel is the story of the ten bridesmaids. As originally told by Jesus, it was most likely a parable. A parable has a single point of comparison. But because the story so closely paralleled the situation in the early Church, as it was passed along in the oral tradition it evolved into an allegory with several points of comparison. To understand the story, we should understand something of the marriage customs in the ancient Near East, why the groom might be delayed, and the role of the bridesmaids.

First of all we should recall that marriages in ancient times were not made in heaven. They were hammered out at a bargaining table by marriage brokers representing the respective families. The bride and groom never met until the actual wedding day. If there were a hitch in the arrangements, particularly over the dowry, the wedding and wedding party could easily be delayed. Second, marriages were often arranged between people from different towns or villages to prevent inbreeding. This meant the groom had to travel a distance at a time when roads were poor, maps non-existent, and means of transportation primitive. All added reasons for delays. Third, marriages were family affairs involving the whole family, from youngest to oldest, from siblings to distant cousins, which in the Mideast would include most of the village. Since all had to travel together for safety and the speed of the caravan was set by the slowest and weakest member, travel time was often prolonged and hard to predict. Still further reason for delay.

As for the bridesmaids, they served both a ceremonial and a practical role. As bridesmaids today, they added beauty and pageantry to the wedding and made it more festive. Even today when a dignitary comes to town, we send a delegation to the airport to greet him and escort him into the city. In similar fashion bridesmaids went out to the city gates to welcome the groom and lead him to the bride's house.

Bridesmaids also served a practical purpose, however. If the groom and his party were coming from another town, they could not be expected to know the area and would need help in finding the bride's home. In those days streets were not laid out in straight lines as they are today, nor did they cross at right angles. They were winding and crooked, frequently mere alleyways leading to dead ends. Bridesmaids were essential as guides, therefore. Also remember that there were no street signs or city maps at the time. People had to know where they were going or rely on someone else to lead them.

Coming from a distance and traveling under uncertain and variable conditions, the groom and his party could well arrive after dark. Ancient cities had no street lights, so the bridesmaids and their torches were a must. Roads were not paved, often in poor repair, and full of ruts and holes. In the dark of night people could easily fall and get hurt. The bridesmaids' torches were essential for the safety of the guests.

In those days people depended on horses, donkeys, and camels for transportation, none of them housebroken. There was also no sanitation department to sweep the streets. So the bridesmaids' torches were also needed to forestall any misstep on the part of a guest and prevent unfortunate consequences. Remember, too, that in those days people wore sandals, their clothes were long and flowing, and the guests could be expected to be decked out in their very finest regalia. Given the number of animals at the time and without a torch to light your way, it would be like walking through a minefield blindfolded. So failure to have one's torch at the ready was a serious violation not only of etiquette, but also of safety, causing embarrassment and loss of face to the bride's family for not fulfilling the customary welcome, and insult and possible injury to the groom's family. The groom clearly had every right to be angry. Grooms were often delayed and the bridesmaids should have been prepared. They were clearly negligent.

When Jesus told the story, it was probably a parable. Jesus compared the audience to the ten virgins and his message was to be prepared. One knows not the day or the hour the Lord will arrive. The early Church, however, saw it as a reflection on their own situation. They believed the Second Coming was imminent, that Jesus would soon return and establish his kingdom. When Jesus did not come, they were confused and saw this story as an allegory containing Jesus' answer for them. God the Father is the one who arranged the marriage, Jesus is the groom, the Christian community is the ten virgins, and the barring of the doors is the Last Judgment. The way for the Church to respond to the delay of the Second Coming was not to grow negligent like the foolish virgins but to always be prepared as the wise virgins.

They also saw symbolism in the oil. Some see those who did not share their oil as uncharitable. But if they divided their oil, all the lamps might have gone out, putting the groom in greater jeopardy. Oil and light, which came from oil lamps, were often used in the Old Testament as symbols for good works. As one cannot attribute one's good deeds to another, so the wise virgins could not share their oil (good works).

Jesus also used the symbolism. "Let your light shine before men so they can see your good deeds" (Mt 5:16). The foolish virgins cry out, "Lord, Lord open the door for us." But Jesus said earlier, "Not everyone who says to me, 'Lord, Lord,' will enter the kingdom of heaven, but only those who do the will of my Father in heaven" (7:21).

While we today don't expect the end of the world any time soon, we know not the day or the hour that God will come for us. So the message is the same. Don't grow negligent or forgetful. Be prepared.

Buried Talent

Suppose you had a son, grandson, or younger brother who was born without a left hand. Assume when he is five or six, he asks you if he'll ever be able to play baseball when he goes to school. What would you tell him? Would you build up his hopes or be realistic? Suppose when watching a baseball game on TV, he asks if he will ever be able to play for the Yankees, if he'll ever be in the starting lineup. How would you answer? Or suppose you had a daughter, granddaughter, or younger sister who lost the front part of her right foot and most of her toes in a freak accident as a toddler. Assume when she is four or five she asks if she'll ever be able to be a ballerina or figure skater. What would you say? And if when entranced by a gold-medal performance by Michelle Kwan she asks if she will ever be able to win a gold medal in figure skating, how would you handle it?

The Abbott family faced the first problem when their son Jim was born without a left hand. I don't know how they fielded his questions as a young boy but I do know that whatever they did they instilled in him the drive and will to succeed despite his considerable handicap. By college Jim was a star athlete, a one-handed pitcher with a record so enviable that the pros came scouting him out. He worked his way up in the big leagues and eventually played several successful seasons for the Yankees where he once pitched a no-hitter. The Zayak family of New Jersey faced the second problem. Their impish daughter Elaine got her foot caught under a lawn mower as a baby. Her family did not allow it to crush her spirit or hopes, however, and she went on to become the first woman ever to land a triple jump in a major figure skating competition and the youngest woman of her time ever to win the U.S. Women's National Championship.

Today's Gospel speaks of developing talents. It tells of a man going on a journey and entrusting to his servants various amounts of money. The money was in talents, which was the largest denomination of money at the time, thus signifying something of inestimable worth. From the Latin word *talentum*, we get our English word "talent" and its connotation provides one interpretation of the story. The man going on the journey is Jesus who will soon ascend into heaven. The servants represent us who are left behind. The point of the story is that we have all been given talents, different gifts and abilities, and God expects us to use them to fashion our world and build up the kingdom of God. God created the universe and set it on its course but part of his plan is for humankind to help shape that world. God expects each of us to use our talents to make the world a better place. We can strive to build a civilization in which all people live as God taught us, as children of God or, through indifference and neglect, we can allow our world to succumb to savagery and selfishness. We can work to protect the earth and render it fruitful, or sit back and let it be laid waste and ruined. God's plan invites us and challenges us to share in the very work of his creation. Failure to cooperate wholeheartedly is a terrible waste and sin.

The servant who received the smallest endowment felt inadequate to the task and went off and buried his talent. He may have been discouraged that the others had much more than he did: one five times more and the other twice as much. But Jesus deliberately used the word "talent" to suggest that even though he only had one talent, it was still a priceless gift because a talent was more than the ordinary person could hope to earn or accumulate in a lifetime. For failing to appreciate his gift and put it to good use in the service of his master, the servant is severely criticized. The point of the different abilities, as symbolized by the different amounts, is that whatever we have by way of God-given gifts are priceless and should be used for God's glory. Not to develop a talent or ourselves to our full ability is to squander God's gifts and not make of ourselves and creation all that God intended us and the world to be.

A talent in ancient times was also used as a symbol for teaching. As valuable coins were handed down from one to another and deeply valued, so were the teachings of religious leaders handed down and esteemed by their followers. In this sense the talents refer to the teaching of Jesus as summed up in the Gospels. The point is that his teachings, like the talents, are not to be buried in the ground but put to use and into practice. As Jesus told us in an earlier parable, we should not bury our faith under a bushel basket but put it on a stand like a light for all to see and to serve as a beacon to draw all people to God.

Like the timid servant many of us feel inadequate to the task of spreading the faith. We ask: who are we and what can we do? We're no Mother Teresa or Fulton Sheen. But there's no need to be. If we think of those who most influenced our faith, it is probably our parents, grandparents, relatives, and friends, none of whom was likely schooled in theology or particularly eloquent. They influenced us simply by the way they lived their faith and put it into practice each day. When we think of it, Mother Teresa taught more by what she did and how she lived than by what she said or wrote and Bishop Sheen's words, for all his eloquence, would have had a hollow ring were it not for the love of God that shone forth in the life he led.

When Jesus speaks of talents, he includes the gift of faith. Those who develop their talents and faith, will see them grow; those who fail to develop their gifts, will see them wither and die. Let us ask God to help us appreciate all the gifts he has given us and help us to develop them to the fullest for his glory.

Separation of Sheep from Goats

Excavators in the Yellow River Valley of China happened upon an incredible treasure trove back in 1974. They unearthed dozens and dozens of true-to-scale terra cotta statues of warriors, horses, and chariots in what proved to be a burial ground over 2000 years old. The treasure which would eventually number some 6000 life-size figures had all been constructed at the order of Emperor Chin to protect him from harm after death. It was the same Emperor Chin who ruled at about the time of Christ and who built the Great Wall of China to protect his country from foreign invaders. The wall, several stories high and stretching a distance of over 3000 miles, still stands today some 2000 years later and is the only human-made structure that astronauts can see unaided from space.

The discovery of the terra cotta figures provoked considerable interest among artists, historians, archeologists, and military scientists. It also caught my attention as a priest. In our world today where the thought of an afterlife and the possibility of a resurrection from the dead are often scoffed at and ridiculed as figments of a Christian imagination, this discovery revealed that 2000 years ago, completely independent of the Judeo-Christian tradition, people believed in an afterlife.

We also know from the pyramids, the tombs of the ancient Egyptian pharaohs, which predate the Christian era by thousands of years and so are free of any Judeo-Christian influence, that the ancient Egyptians also believed in an afterlife. The pharaohs were buried with inestimable treasures of gold and precious jewelry, as it was felt that life in the next world was much like life in this one.

Even in the Americas, in the Aztec and Mayan cultures, more than a thousand years ago, long before Christianity ever reached our shores, people buried their dead with bowls and eating utensils. Simple people, inured to a hand-to-mouth existence, they too believed in an afterlife and obviously tried to provide the wherewithal for their dead to eat there.

With numerous indications from history over many millennia that people of very different cultures from all over the world believed in an afterlife but were confused as to its nature, we should be grateful as Christians for the revelation that Jesus has given us. Jesus has assured us that we have a loving Father in heaven and that he, Jesus, has gone ahead to prepare a place for us. In today's Gospel, he also tells us the conditions for entrance into heaven, removing the doubts and fears of people from other cultures and civilizations. We do not need an army, as Emperor Chin feared. We do not need wealth, as the Egyptians believed. Though Jesus often compared heaven to a banquet, we do not have to provide our own utensils as the Mayans and Aztecs thought. Our entrance into heaven will depend only on our conduct, our love for God and neighbor as evidenced by the good we did or failed to do during our lifetime. For Jesus tells us quite simply in today's Gospel that whatever we do to the least of our brothers and sisters, that he considers as done to himself. If we are to gain access to heaven, we have simply to love God and all he has created.

Today's Gospel is in many ways surprising. As we enter the third millennium since the birth of Christ, it is interesting to note that God will not judge the world by the rise and fall of nations or civilizations, nor by the outcomes of major wars or revolutions, nor by the discovery of new worlds or planets, nor by the inventions of science or technology, but by the simple acts of love performed one for another and often so inconspicuous by nature that those performing the acts are unaware of their significance. It is also interesting to note that the characters in the story are not surprised by the need to show love for others but by the need to show love even for the least in society.

The Gospel today may also catch some by surprise for it shows God as a God of justice. Too often we concentrate on the notion of a loving God who will do all to save humankind but we forget that there is a limit to God's patience and the time allotted any one individual. Today's Gospel warns us that when time runs out, God will act decisively. Those who have not responded to his love for them by showing love for others in their lifetime, will be banished from his sight and cut off from his love forever. This in itself is a condition far worse than any hell fire we could ever imagine.

Today's Gospel is at once consoling and challenging. It is consoling because it tells us we do not have to do anything extraordinary to enter heaven. God takes all that we do for others as done to himself. Having recently celebrated the Feast of All Saints, we should recall the many acts of kindness our deceased relatives and friends performed for us during their lifetime and ask God to reward them now by welcoming them into the company of his saints in heaven. It is also challenging, however, because it reminds us that time is limited and we have much yet to show of our love for God and others. Let us pray that we not waste precious time or opportunities.